Reforming the Secret State

Studies in Law and Politics

Published by Open University Press in association with the
Centre for Socio-Legal Studies

Reforming the Secret State

by

Professor Patrick Birkinshaw

Edited by

Norman Lewis, Cosmo Graham and Deryck Beyleveld

Open University Press
Milton Keynes - Philadelphia

Open University Press
Celtic Court
22 Ballmoor
Buckingham MK18 1XW

and

1900 Frost Road, Suite 101
Bristol, PA 19007, USA

First Published

British Library Cataloguing in Publication Data
Birkinshaw, Patrick.
Reforming the Secret State - (Studies in Law and Politics)
1. Great Britain. Official secrets. Disclosure. Law.
Official Secrets Acts 1911. Reform
I. Title. II. Series
344.10523
ISBN 0-335-09631-X

Library of Congress Cataloguing-in-Publication Data
Birkinshaw, Patrick.
Reforming the Secret State/Patrick Birkinshaw.
p. cm. -- (Studies in Law and Politics)
Includes index.
ISBN 0-335-09631-X (pbk.)
1. Freedom of Information -- Great Britian. 2. Government
Information -- Great Britian. 3. Official Secrets -- Great Britain.
I. Title. II. Series.
KD 3756.B57 1990
342.41 0662 -- dc20
[344.102662]
                                                    90-21662 CIP
Printed in Great Britain by J.W. Arrowsmith Limited, Bristol

Contents

Editorial Introduction

Norman Lewis

Although the second title in the series, this is the first full monograph to emerge. Patrick Birkinshaw's earlier work on freedom of information and governmental secrecy will already be known to many of our readers and this latest contribution will not disappoint his many admirers.

In the spirit of the series, this monograph ranges much wider than merely providing an analysis of the Official Secrets and Security Service Acts 1989, though a scholarly analysis is certainly provided. Not only is the background to the legislation discussed but it is set in the broader context of democratic expectations; in the context of the role of information in a free society. This is largely achieved through a rigorous analysis of Freedom of Information and Privacy laws in the United States Federal experience. I was personally witness to the enormous body of contacts which Patrick Birkinshaw made within the Federal Administration two years ago, from the CIA and the Pentagon through the Office of Manpower and Budget to the Federal Communications Commission. This is testament not only to his talents as an empirical researcher, but also to the nature of American public life itself where a culture of openness contrasts so starkly with British experience. The casual visitor to Washington D.C. cannot fail to be struck by the ease with which they can inspect the chambers of the Senate and the House on an ordinary Sunday afternoon. It is the people's government and so they naturally possess it. The U.S. visitor to Britain cannot but be amazed at their inability to do the same in the Houses of Parliament. Their amazement is increased by the fact that the ordinary Briton accepts the position so philosophically.

There is then, an enormous difference of approach between the two countries when it comes to the business of open government. The whole Spycatcher saga in Britain was a shameful episode which made our institutions of government look more than faintly ridiculous around the world. Our Parliamentary system appeared foolish and inadequate; our system of executive government was shown to be high-handed, imperious and unresponsive, and our judiciary biddable and pusillanimous. The result has been a woefully inadequate public debate concerning what information ought to be put in the public domain and that which actually needs to be restrained in the interests of effective government. Our political institutions (the unfashionable Royal Commission apart) are not noted for their encouragement of genuine discourse or informed dissent, and the two Acts of Parliament which this monograph concentrates upon emerged out of a system which has been largely discredited and which, unsurprisingly, produced reform of the three steps forward and two and a half backwards variety. Indeed, on one interpretation, the hand of the executive has been considerably strengthened during the course of this legislative 'advance'.

What is more to the point, as Professor Birkinshaw makes clear, is that the new legislation is pragmatic, incremental and disingenuous and seeks nowhere to talk the language of first principles; except perhaps the unspoken one that government knows best. For many years British government has refused to heed lessons from abroad on the basis that, as far as Continental Europe was concerned, a civil law system was untransplantable, and, as far as the United States was concerned, the absence of a Westminster system of government made comparisons fanciful and unconstructive. The major changes which have occurred over the last decade or so in the 'old' commonwealth (Canada, Australia and New Zealand) have simply been ignored. The position adopted in the monograph is that we cannot continue to be out of step for very much longer and still play an active part in a community of free nations. In time, Freedom of Information (FOI) will come to Britain as it has to so many other countries, and when it does we shall need to absorb the lessons which have been learned elsewhere. Patrick Birkinshaw has examined the American experience in order to pose questions and suggest solutions for consideration in a British policy debate on FOI as and when it comes. American experience is the longest in this area and certainly the most judiciary-dependent. I believe that Professor Birkinshaw is right to argue that, at the end of the day, constitutional reform is ultimately dependent upon the courts of law and upon legal autonomy. It is not an argument that is currently fashionable but it is part of a debate which we need to have as a nation. FOI is a *sine qua non* of a democratic system of government. So is an independent judiciary. It is certainly possible to argue that, at the moment, we possess neither. It is not an argument that I am personally convinced by, but I have no doubt that we should be entertaining a great constitutional debate. *Reforming the Secret State* is a valuable contribution to that debate and Patrick Birkinshaw has provided a service in making it.

Preface

I would like to thank the British Academy, the US Government, and the Sir Philip Reckitt Research Trust for supporting the research which led to the present work. In particular I would like to thank R.L. Huff and D.J. Metcalfe of the US Department of Justice; G.J. Edles of the Administrative Conference of the US; P. Moschella of the FBI; J.H. Wright of the CIA; W.M. McDonald, C. Talbott and A. Nepa Jnr. of the Department of Defense; R.C. Hardzog of the Defense Intelligence Agency; and the relevant section heads in the Securities and Exchange Commission, the Environmental Protection Agency, the Department of Health and Social Services, the Consumer Product Safety Commission and the Office of Management and Budget. I would also like to thank R. Gellman, Staff Director of the House Government Information, Justice and Agriculture Subcommittee, and Dr H. Relyea of the Congressional Research Service; Patti Goldman of the Public Interest Litigation Group: D. Sobel of the National Security Archive; R. Roberts of the American Society of Access Professionals; and Harry Hammitt of Access Reports. Dr. Relyea was of enormous assistance in organising my research trip to the USA and providing guidance on the law. Needless to say, I alone bear sole responsibility for the contents and views expressed herein.

The US component of the study comprised detailed discussions with the senior officials responsible for FOIA (Freedom of

Information Act) and PA (Privacy Act) administration in a wide variety of government departments and agencies as listed above.

Detailed responses were also received from the heads of those sections responsible for FOIA and PA administration in the CIA and the Consumer Product Safety Commission. The research is based partly upon the comments of officials which were on the record and also upon official documentation which they supplied, most of which is publicly available.

I would also like to thank Professor Norman Lewis and Cosmo Graham for their helpful advice and criticism.

Abstract

The burden of the following monograph is that the reforms in our secrecy laws, the Official Secrets Act and the Security Service Act of 1989, are far from the liberalising measures so lauded by the government. The Official Secrets Act, replacing the notorious Section 2 of the Act of 1911, was described by the Home Secretary as 'an essay in openness unparalleled since the Second World War'. The Act says not one word about greater provision of information to the public. It is true that the ambit of official information covered by the criminal law under the Act has been restricted. However, new statutory provisions have been introduced to plug some of the gaps, and the civil service disciplinary code has been amended to cover a wider range of information. Interpreting the difficult provisions of the Act will be a daunting task for those who operate in the information business. The absolute, or very wide, nature of some offences, making successful prosecution an easier task for the state, will inhibit publication and discussion. With the Security Service Act, the government has enacted the absolute minimum safeguard to make the operations of the security service 'answerable' to the executive rather than to representatives in the elected chamber.

Critics of the secret state in Britain frequently make comparison with the freedom of information (FOI) legislation of the United States, or Commonwealth countries. Advocates for open government argue for legislation on the American or some other model. But how does freedom of information actually operate? Who uses it and why? What difficulties are caused by its introduction and what alterations and what accompanying changes in administrative practice and culture are necessitated? Arguing for a Freedom of Information Act (FOIA) for central government in the United Kingdom, the monograph offers analysis and tentative suggestions for some of the above problems by examining the operation and administration of the US FOIA.

Reforming the Secret State

Introduction

It will cause little surprise that the 1980s, the decade of reform, would see an eventual recasting of Section 2 of the Official Secrets Act (OSA) 1911. Within months of first taking office in 1979, Mrs. Thatcher had attempted to replace Section 2 with a Protection of Official Information Act. Her customary luck abandoned her in those early days. The revelations surrounding Sir Anthony Blunt, the 'spy in the Palace', and his role in the seemingly unending Burgess, Mclean, Philby *et al.* saga compelled the government to withdraw the Bill from the Lords when the press recognised that the Bill was more repressive than Section 2. If enacted, it would have criminalised the disclosures of the Blunt affair itself, which included a secret 'pardon' from an unidentified source allowing Blunt to continue as an adviser to the Queen. Successive Prime Ministers pleaded ignorance of these events.

Governments had confronted difficulties with official secrecy long, long before the first OSA statute of 1889 (Birkinshaw 1988). Section 2 of the 1911 Act had seemingly given the government what it wanted; a catch-all criminal provision punishing unauthorised leaks and receipt of official information in Kafkaesque terms. However, in spite of Section 2's brooding presence the very breadth and lack of definition provided defence lawyers with opportunities to weave uncertainties in jurors' minds, to question suggestively the real interests of the state and to persuade juries to return verdicts against an over-mighty and arrogant executive.

Clive Ponting's acquittal from charges under Section 2 in 1985 (*R v. Ponting* [1985] Crim. L.R. 318), to almost universal public acclaim, persuaded the Government that Section 2 could not remain unaltered. The Spycatcher litigation (*A-G v. Guardian Newspapers Ltd* [1987] 3 All ER 316; and (No 2) [1988] 3 All ER 545) exposed holes in the law which needed plugging. But Tory MP Richard Shepherd's Private Member's Bill, which sought to replace Section 2 with a liberalising measure, forced action upon the government. The Bill evoked the traditional double standards over the need for secrecy in government with the invocation by the Prime Minister of a three-line whip and the pay-roll to suppress support for the Bill among Tory MPs. By June 1988, a White Paper on the reform of Section 2 had been published (Cm. 408). An Official Secrets Bill was presented to the Commons in November 1988, and the Royal Assent was conferred in May 1989. In the preceding month, the Security Service Bill, which placed MI5 on a statutory footing, was assented to. That Bill's advent had not been preceded by any officially published papers.

Thus the Government sought to strike a balance between the need to protect critical secrets and 'the public's right to know how their government works', and to give a legal basis to its security service, especially its intrusions into individuals' privacy. Urging caution, opposition MPs found out that in the case of the Official Secrets Act, the Government was legislating not for the next five years, but for the next generation. In my view, however, both statutes are no more than staging posts to fuller and more meaningful reform of official secrecy and greater openness in our government. I shall explain why I believe that to be the case.

The Background to Reform

More ink has probably been spilled on Section 2 OSA than on any other statutory provision in British law. Since 1972, it has been the subject of three separate command papers, the first of which came in four volumes (Cm. 5104 (1972); Cm. 7285 (1978); Cm. 408 (1988)). The section has received constant attention from the press, media, and academic commentators. It was also almost universally misunderstood; a position which until the 1970s suited successive governments. Indeed the White Paper of 1988 continued the misunderstanding by referring to the penalising of disclosures of 'any' information. (Cm. 408: para.8.) First, it is worth remarking that ignorance of the law was no defence; again very convenient for incumbent governments and especially dangerous for such a capricious 'catch-all' law. A brief history of Section 2 will probably be helpful (Williams 1965; Birkinshaw 1988).

The OSA 1911 replaced the Act of 1889, the latter of which had proved deficient for prosecutors. Section 1 of the 1911 Act provides penalties for spying, although its operation has been extended by judicial decision beyond the field of espionage. (*Chandler v. DPP* [1962] 3 All ER 142). A draft of what was to become Section 2 had been in preparation for several years, the government awaiting a suitable opportunity to introduce it into Parliament. In August 1911, that opportunity presented itself. Britain was gripped by hysteria and fear over the might of the German state and by preoccupation with espionage. Thus the Bill was introduced and passed through all its stages in the House of Commons within twenty four hours without opposition. There were some protests, but 'the general response was one of unspoken loyalty' (Williams 1965: 26). It remained the law of the land for almost seventy-nine years.

Putting it simply, it provided that any person communicating information as categorised in any one of five ways was guilty of an offence under Section 2(1). Section 2(2) also created an offence for the unauthorised receipt of the information protected under Section 2(1) (Birkinshaw 1988: 76-82). Receipt under Section 2(2) required *mens rea*, a lawyers expression for a 'guilty' mind while under Section 2(1) it did not; or so the better opinion had it.

Table 1
Official Secrets Act 1911 Section 2
England and Wales

No. of persons prosecuted in Magistrates' courts.

	1985	1986	1987	1988
No. prosecuted	5	0	3	10
Discharged	2	0	0	0
Committed for trial	3	0	2	10
Found guilty	0	0	1	0
No of persons prosecuted in Crown Court				
	1985	1986	1987	1988
No. of persons for trial	2	3	4	6
Found guilty	0	2	3	3

(Figures kindly supplied by the Home Office).

There was also the widest provision for the punishment of aiding, abetting, inciting and attempt. Numerous prosecutions, which had to be authorised by the Attorney-General, were brought under its provisions. Since 1985, the year of Ponting's trial, the number of prosecutions brought under Section 2 are shown in Table 1.

The trial of Johnathan Aitken in 1971, and his subsequent acquittal, are regarded as turning points in the section's life (Aitken 1971), and in 1972 Franks produced his much quoted report on Section 2 (Franks 1972). Although he found understanding of the section to be limited, he nevertheless criticised its draconian nature. Franks recommended reform that would punish disclosures causing at least serious injury in a limited number of areas.[1] He had no doubt that the criminal law was needed to punish unauthorised leaks outside the area of espionage under Section 1, but believed that the law needed to be better focussed. He also recommended the use of a ministerial certificate for the court to certify, as conclusive evidence, that documents were appropriately classified as secret and confidential at the time of an offence and that unauthorised disclosure would cause serious injury. These recommendations were not pursued by the government of the day although their contents have continued to inform the subsequent debate.

Following the conviction of three defendants in the so-called 'ABC' trial in 1978 under various provisions relating to communicating and receiving information which was otherwise publicly available (Aubrey 1981), the Callaghan Government published a White Paper on Section 2 in 1978 (Cm. 7285). In fact, a Freedom of Information Bill was at committee stage in the Commons when the government lost a vote of confidence resulting in the dissolution of Parliament. Mrs. Thatcher's first abortive efforts at reform, on the other hand, have already been referred to.

While Mrs. Thatcher has always maintained that she has been more forthcoming on national security information that any preceding Prime Minister, she has throughout her premiership been preoccupied by secrecy and national security. This preoccupation was fostered by the influence of her close friendship with Airey Neave MP who was murdered by Irish terrorists in 1979. While this is understandable, the Prime Minister has also been avidly opposed to a freedom of information act (FOIA) affecting central government. In spite of her zealous profession of a minimal state, her obsession with a strong state in the area of secrecy has shown her government not only in its most unattractive guise but also in its most vindictive and silliest.

 The Sarah Tisdall case in 1983 revealed the vindictive streak particularly forcefully. Tisdall, a junior official in the Ministry of Defence, leaked documents to the Guardian which showed that Michael Heseltine, the Secretary of State for Defence, was misleadingly holding back information from Parliament on the timing of the arrival of the first Cruise missiles to Britain. There were no reasons of national security for the delay; it was merely an attempt to outflank the opposition. Rather than contesting the case, Sarah Tisdall confessed and pleaded guilty. Her imprisonment for what had, she claimed, been an act of conscience evoked strong waves of sympathy. For Lord Beloff, however, she was a 'muddle-headed young idealist female' (505 HL Debs, col. 922, 3 April 1989).

The Ponting episode (*R v. Ponting* [1985] Crim. L.R. 318) was one of two cases that was to prove catastrophic. Ponting was a senior civil servant whose responsibilities within the Ministry of Defence included the policy and political aspects of the operational activities of the Royal Navy. While engaged on drafting replies on questions relating to the sinking of the Belgrano by the Royal Navy in the Falklands hostilities, he leaked information showing that the Government was misleading the House of Commons, a select committee and the public over the events leading to the loss of 368 lives.[2] No national security risk was present in the leak but Ponting was arrested, charged and tried for an offence under Section 2(1). To general amazement, he was acquitted (Ponting 1985). Presumably the jury must have accepted that what Ponting had done had been performed as a duty 'in the interests of the state'. This was in spite of a vigorous judicial direction to the jury to the contrary which equated the interests of the state with the interests of the government of the day. An authorisation to disseminate could only come from within the official chain of command. Ponting's acquittal brought home dramatically the unreliability of Section 2 when the government might wish to use it most: to stifle a well motivated act of conscience causing the government acute embarrassment.

The Spycatcher litigation, on the other hand, exposed the yawning gaps in our official secrecy laws from the government's perspective. It was also an unnecessarily silly episode. Peter Wright, a somewhat embittered former MI5 agent, had published his memoirs through an Australian branch of a publishing house, after the British government had unsuccessfully attempted to stop publication in Australia. The book contained certain serious allegations against MI5 officers which had been well rehearsed by other authors. They included allegations of treason. Although important items of some of Wright's claims were subsequently shown to be unreliable, the allegations of treason have been separately supported by a former member of army intelligence operating in Ulster, Colin Wallace. However until early 1990, Prime Ministerial inquiries had not, we are informed, established any supporting evidence.

It is worth noting that because Wright was outside the jurisdiction, Section 2 was unavailable to the government. The Attorney-General as law officer of the Crown therefore resorted to the civil law of confidentiality. That the civil law could be moulded to protect the secrets of the state and its servants as well as the confidences of private individuals had been apparent from the judgment of Lord Widgery CJ in *A-G v. Jonathan Cape* ([1976] QB 752). The weapon employed by the court to maintain an existing confidence in the event of a threatened breach is an interlocutory injunction. Where the court wishes to maintain confidentiality in a state or a private individual's secret, the injunction performs a 'prior restraint'; an act of censorship in order to maintain the status quo pending a final hearing. A defendant may raise a variety of defences in the interlocutory proceedings including a public interest defence, which I discuss below. However, the onus on the defendant is a very heavy one since once the possibility of a duty of confidence is found to exist, a judge will want to be convinced that such a defence will succeed at the final hearing for a permanent injunction. Given that framework, and in the absence of a constitutional First Amendment guaranteeing freedom of speech as in the USA, an interlocutory injunction will invariably be issued to maintain a confidential relationship where a putative confidence can still be protected.

So it was that several newspapers found themselves enjoined from publishing any information from Wright's book since, as a former 'insider', a strong presumption of confidence could be inferred. They were also enjoined from reporting in the UK the proceedings in New South Wales taken by the Court to prevent publication of Spycatcher, even though the proceedings were in open court. Incredibly, the Law Lords even had to be advised that they lacked the power to prohibit the reporting of the proceedings of the British House of Commons concerning Wright's allegations. By the time of the interlocutory decision in the House of Lords, Spycatcher, the book was widely available in the UK having been published in the USA and elsewhere. The decision of the majority of Law Lords provoked Lord Bridge, a dissenting Law Lord and former chairman of the Security Commission, to inveigh against the pusillanimity of English law in its failure to protect the freedom of the press and to declare the need for fundamental safeguards ([1987] 3 All ER at 346). Such criticism was redoubled when contempt proceedings were successfully brought against other newspapers, not named in the original order, prohibiting publication when they had published stories based on the contents of Spycatcher (*A-G v. Newspaper Publishing Ltd* [1987] 3 All ER 276).

On the plus side, the judgment of Scott J. in the proceedings for a permanent injunction in December 1987, did much to restore the judicial reputation (*A-G v. Guardian Newspapers* (No.2) [1988] 3 All ER 545). Scott J. refused to award permanent injunctions prohibiting the press reporting the contents of Spycatcher and the account of proceedings in the Australian courts. Even Spycatcher itself could be published because it was in the public domain, although not by Wright or his publishers. The judgment emphasised, and this was supported by the higher courts, that injunctions would not be awarded to protect confidential information entrusted to or possessed by Crown servants unless publication would damage the public interest. The onus was on the Crown to establish that the information was confidential and that publication would damage the public interest. Where all the damage had already been done, an injunction would not be awarded. It was accepted and subsequently re-emphasised (*Lord Advocate v. Scotsman Publishing Ltd* [1989] 2 All ER 852) that security and intelligence officers owe a life-long duty of confidentiality. Scott J.'s judgment, which was upheld on appeal by the Court of Appeal and House of Lords, contains many features which require addressing. It must be remembered, however, that this judgment faces the argument at the stage of a permanent injunction, not an interlocutory one; i.e. the stage of 'prior restraint' in the latter case.

For the government then the case revealed fatal flaws in the law, and proposals were prepared to deal with them. Before their release, the government information network sedulously planted stories of tyrannical attempts by the government itself to protect all official information by a life-long duty of confidentiality (*The Sunday Times* 12 June 1988). The publication of the White Paper on Reform of Section 2 of the Official Secrets Act 1911 (Cm. 408) was therefore greeted with welcome surprise by the press who at first saw it as a liberalising measure (*The Times* 30 June 1988). The paper was cleverly drafted so that only those well versed in secrecy laws would be able to see through its facade. Faced by challenges before the European Commission of Human Rights over the operation of MI5, the Government also decided to establish a minimal statutory framework for the Security Service. In fact, the Commission of Human Rights and Council of Ministers subsequently decided that breaches of Articles 8 and 13 had occurred in MI5 activities (*The Independent* 24 April 1990).

The White Paper

The fourteen page White Paper took fourteen months to complete. Its theme was the Franks view that Section 1 OSA does not provide full protection for official information and that the criminal law needs to punish leakage as well as espionage where there is a sufficient degree of harm to the public interest. The White Paper said nothing about the 'separate issue' of freedom of information or provision of information because this did not arise directly out of the reform of Section 2. It is therefore difficult to square with the Home Secretary's subsequent statements that his Bill represented a 'substantial unprecedented thrust in the direction of greater openness', that it was an 'essay in openness' ..... 'unprecedented since the Second World War'.

The government ultimately decided not to follow Franks but to 'look afresh at the issues', taking into account the criticisms of its 1979 Bill and the development of Parliamentary and public thinking in recent years. A closer look at such thinking would suggest that the government had been treating it less than sympathetically.

Six specific areas of information were to be protected against unauthorised disclosure where the disclosure was damaging. Damaging disclosures by unauthorised recipients would be covered, but the mere receipt of official information without authority was not to be a crime unless, presumably, aiding and abetting, incitement or conspiracy could be charged. However, the White Paper dropped the idea of ministerial certificates which specified that the information was properly classified as information the disclosure of which was considered likely to cause serious injury to the interests of the nation. In Shepherd's Bill, ministerial certificates were to remain, but they were to be subject to challenge before the Judicial Committee of the Privy Council. The new requirement that a disclosure be 'damaging' was less onerous than the 'serious damage' requirement of the 1979 Bill, although in that Bill serious injury was to be established by a ministerial certificate. The White Paper stipulated that there was to be no public interest defence as had been present in the Shepherd Bill, nor a defence of prior publication, even though one had been present in clause 7(1) of the 1979 Bill.

Although disclosures had normally to be proved to be damaging by the prosecution, there were four areas where the disclosure would *ipso facto* be deemed damaging, and where UK interests abroad were concerned the disclosure only had to jeopardise or seriously obstruct those interests. The first covered leaks by security and intelligence officials and notified persons of security and intelligence information. The second absolute offence concerned the disclosure of information obtained or information concerning activities under the Interception of Communications Act 1985 and what was to be the Security Service Act 1989, i.e. burglary and 'investigations' by MI5. These would cover Ponting, Peter Wright and Cathy Massiter, the former MI5 official who disclosed that CND's telephone lines and those of its members were being tapped (see *R v. Secretary of State for the Home Department ex p. Ruddock* [1987] 2 All ER 518). The third area covered information relating to international relations. Fourthly, information obtained in confidence from other governments would be protected - it seemed absolutely - as any disclosure without authority would be harmful. Information would also be protected when given in confidence to a foreign government, but only where it was leaked without authority in that state and subsequently published in the UK. The Act provided for the protection of information relating to defence and that which would be useful to criminals if disclosed without authority. These were the fifth and sixth categories of protected information.

> The government .... proposes that, when it is necessary for the courts to consider the harm likely to arise from the disclosure of particular information, the prosecution should be required to adduce evidence as to that harm and the defence should be free to produce its own evidence in rebuttal. The burden of proof would be on the prosecution in the normal way. (Cm. 408: para. 18)

In other words, no ministerial certificates would dictate to the jury a finding of guilt. A free trial before one's peers, recently so lauded by the remnants of the liberal press during Ponting's acquittal, was to be preserved in all its integrity. The fact that the ground rules determined that no likely defence was available for certain disclosures was beside the point. But it is disingenuous to state, as we shall see, that ministerial certificates have not been introduced.

There were, nevertheless, certain improvements. Large areas of official information would no longer be covered by the Official Secrets Acts. For example, cabinet documents were not to be protected as a class unless they fell within one of the above protected categories. Economic information was not to be protected as a class (e.g. the budget), and information given to government in confidence was not to be protected *per se*. The information would have to fall within one of the six categories. The White Paper indicated that, at the same time, civil service rules and departmental rules would be amended to make new provision for internal disciplinary punishment to protect information not covered by the OSA. New statutes would also provide for criminal offences for unauthorised disclosure as and when required. In 1987, the number of such statutes extended to 137 (108 HC Debs, cols. 560 - 2, 21 January 1987, Written Answers). New ones have since been added and I shall have more to say on this matter.

contained a public interest defence where the defendant had
However, it is deceptive, therefore, to assert as the White Paper does
that the 'result of implementing the Government's proposals would be
that only small proportions of the information in the hands of Crown
servants would be protected by the criminal law' (para. 71).

Classification of information for security purposes still remains,
even though classification at a particular grade of secrecy is not, of
itself, evidence of likely harm or damage in a court of law.
Classification will continue to play an 'essential administrative role in
the handling of information' within government itself and will also be
relevant for internal disciplinary offences. In a criminal trial, a
classification will not be evidence of the causing of damage; but the
grade may be relevant 'as evidence tending to show that the defendant
had reason to believe that the disclosure of the information was likely
to harm the public interest'. The causation of damage will have to be
proved by separate evidence. Classifications, which are reviewable
internally, are as follows (Franks 1972: paras. 62-3):

Where classified as 'Top Secret', official opinion believes
publication or disclosure without authority would cause exceptionally
grave damage to the nation. This is the most important class of
information.

'Secret' covers information where unauthorised publication etc.
would cause serious injury to the interests of the nation. It is not as
important as 'Top Secret'.

'Confidential' as a classification is given where publication etc.
would be prejudicial to the interests of the nation. All that can be said
is that the distinction between 'serious injury' and 'prejudicial' is very
much a matter for the eye of the beholder.

Lastly, and not really secret at all, comes 'Restricted', where
publication would be undesirable in the interests of the nation. There
are privacy markings and these cover:

'Commercial - in confidence', 'Management - in confidence'
(presumably organisational information), and 'Staff - in confidence'
(presumably personnel information). It should be pointed out that in
this context 'Confidential means secret'.

The burden and quantum of proof would vary as between civil
servants/government contractors and civilians. Among civil servants,
where the offence related to security and intelligence information, a
distinction was drawn between security and intelligence officials and
'notified' officials in one group and other civil servants in another.
Unauthorised disclosures by the former group are, in the absence of
one unlikely defence which I will discuss below, an absolute offence.
For other offences, a distinction was drawn between civil servants

government contractors) and civilians. The test of liability would depend upon the state of knowledge of the discloser, and in the case of Crown Servants it is reasonable to assume that they know the value of the information received in official duties. *Mens rea* is also a component of the offence. It would be open to the civil servant or contractor to plead that they could not reasonably have been expected to realise the harm likely to be caused by the disclosure. In the case of civilians, the opposite presumption would be made, and the prosecution should have to prove that harm was likely to follow and that the discloser knew, or could be reasonably expected to know, that harm would be likely to result. The constituents of the prosecution case differ according to the category of defendant. In the case of civil servants and contractors, *mens rea* is presumed unless proved otherwise; in the case of civilians, knowledge of the damaging quality has to be established by the prosecution. In the case of information obtained under interception or security warrants, once the prosecution has established that a non-civil servant knew, or had reasonable cause to believe that, it was such information and that it was disclosed unlawfully under the Act, the offence is made out.

Reference must be made to the special treatment of classes of security and intelligence information. Because it would normally be necessary for the prosecution to present additional evidence that such disclosures were damaging to secure a conviction, the Government declared that further and possibly greater damage could be caused by adducing such information. To counter such difficulty, it was proposed that the prosecution could show that the information disclosed was of a class or description the disclosure of which would be likely to damage the operation of the services. 'This would allow the arguments to be less specific' (Cm. 408: para. 40). We should be clear about what this means. The prosecution would simply assert that the information belongs to a class of information the disclosure of which is damaging. No specific supporting evidence would have to be produced. It is difficult to interpret this as anything other than a ministerial certificate which the White Paper had appeared to rule out. Granted that this is restricted to one category of information, nevertheless the continued classification of documents and the secret lists of ministerially designated and 'notified' officials who work in close proximity with the security and intelligence services has to be appreciated.

Public Interest Disclosure

The White Paper adverted specifically to the defences of prior publication and public interest disclosure. The Shepherd Bill had reasonable cause to believe crime, fraud, abuse of authority, neglect, or other misconduct had been perpetrated. The judicially developed law of confidentiality has long recognised that there cannot be a confidence in an iniquity (*Gartside v. Outram* (1856) 26 LJ Ch. 113). A duty cannot be owed to maintain as a secret that which ought, in the public interest, to be disclosed. The courts have come to accept that a disclosure may be justified not because there is an iniquity but because there is an item of information the disclosure of which is justified on the facts (*Lion Laboratories v. Evans* [1984] 3 WLR 539). The public interest defence was dramatically invoked by Scott J. in Spycatcher when he held that the revelations of Wright's allegations, concerning the attempts to undermine the Wilson government and the plot to assassinate President Nasser by MI5 and MI6 officials, respectively, were protected by a public interest defence. Correspondingly, the press were justified in publishing this information, at least in its essentials. This was information which the idea of democracy demanded should be placed before the public. Scott J. suggested that revelations by an official may also be so protected, in spite of the life-long duty of confidentiality, a point supported by the higher courts. However, since the security allegations formed a minute part of the book, Wright has been culpable in publishing the book in that particular form. What this amounted to was that, in examining the public interest defence, the court will look very carefully at the manner and method of disclosure, and the motives of the discloser. Financial gain and widespread publication may undermine the defence so that the prudent course of action might be to inform the police or Solicitor-General rather than the press. This latter point has been emphasised by Lord Donaldson MR on a variety of occasions, as well as by Lord Griffiths and Goff in Spycatcher.

In Canada, public servants at the federal level may successfully invoke the public interest defence against disciplinary hearings (Quigley v Treasury Board [1987] Public Service Staff Relations Board 166-2-16866). No such allowance is made for British civil servants. The defence is only a defence against a civil action for breach of confidence, and the confider still retains his or her rights under the law of employment, a position complicated in the UK by the uncertain status of civil servants who appear not to possess enforceable contracts of employment (*R v. Civil Service Appeal Board ex p. Bruce* [1989] 2 All ER 907). It is worth making the point that those who 'whistleblow' in the public interest in the UK subsequently fare very badly (Cripps 1987; Winfield 1990). This is little less than disgraceful. As we shall see below, US civil servants possess a 'Whistleblower's charter' to protect them against administrative reprisals.

The government refused to countenance a public interest defence which would allow juries to consider and balance the benefits of the unauthorised disclosure of information, the motives of the discloser, and the harm it was likely to cause. Several attempts to introduce such defences in the Commons and Lords failed. It was the government's line that the object of reform of Section 2 had been to introduce clarity, and that such a defence would subvert this aim. Further, the reforms would concentrate on protecting areas of information which demonstrably require the protection of the criminal law 'in the public interest'. The government argued: 'It cannot be acceptable that a person can lawfully disclose information which he knows may, for example, lead to loss of life simply because he conceives that he has a general reason of a public character for doing so' (Cm. 408: para. 60). This seems to me to confuse an assertion of such a defence by a defendant with its acceptance by a jury. Expressed in the government's terms, the claim sounds startling. The public interest defence allows a defendant to plead that the disclosure has been a positive benefit to the public interest. It is not a licence for the mischievous, the woolly-headed and loose-tongued. The idea is to let the jury decide where there are arguments of damage and benefit. Yet the government would not contemplate such a contest: 'the effect of disclosure on the public interest should take place within the context of the proposed damage tests where applicable' (Cm. 408: para. 61). The government's one assurance, binding in honour only, was that the Act would not be used to punish those who had embarrassed the government. However, if an offence has been committed there is no provision for juries to be instructed according to the government's assurance. Only a 'perverse' jury could, therefore, save a defendant who had acted in the public interest out of conscience. The jury that acquitted Ponting was not, arguably, perverse in that it felt, presumably, that he had acted 'in the interests of the state'. A powerful argument can be made out to the effect that for a jury to acquit in such circumstances is not a perverse action but a rational one motivated by integrity (MacCormick 1986). However, such a defence is no longer available. It is merely a question of the prosecutor's discretion, a matter which highlights the long-running problem over the Attorney-General's independence from Government colleagues (Ponting 1985; Nicol 1979).

The government's continued claim that a public interest defence had no respectable precedent in our criminal law is also unfounded.

As well as a generic defence of 'necessity', specific statutes may contain such defences.

Prior Publication

The White Paper ruled out the necessity of a prior publication defence, arguing that the inclusion of such a defence in the 1979 Bill was 'flawed' (cf. Section 180(1) (r) Financial Services Act 1986, which allows a defence of prior publication[3]). The government's case, also argued with success before the courts (*Lord Advocate v. Scotsman*), was that a further publication of information already in the public domain might be damaging, possibly even more damaging than the original publication. A newspaper story about a certain matter may carry little weight in the absence of firm evidence of its validity. But confirmation of that story by, say, a senior official of the relevant government department would be very much more damaging and deserving of prosecution. So would publication of details of 'persons in public life' in one list, even though the names and addresses were publicly, albeit not conveniently, available elsewhere (Cm. 408: para 62.). Prior publication would be relevant to assess the degree of harm, and it is therefore possible to argue that the damage alleged had already been perpetrated. But prior publication would not be conclusive for the defence. In some cases, viz. security and intelligence and interception and security warrant cases, prior publication would be irrelevant as the offences are 'absolute'. Case law suggests that prior publication without government action to prevent publication may indicate that disclosure has been authorised, even though the information is still technically 'secret' (*R v. Galvin* [1987] 2 All ER 851).

The House of Lords (*Lord Advocate v. Scotsman*) accepted the thrust of government thinking, when it acknowledged that the test for awarding an injunction to prevent publication in the law of confidentiality, was that if an injunction were not awarded there would be damage or further damage to the public interest. If the test is satisfied, an injunction may be awarded even where the information or document has been published on a limited basis. In the case in question it was only the government admission that all the damage had already occurred that prevented the award of the injunction. On the other hand, government attempts to stifle what had already been widely published had met with the rebuke from Lord Griffiths, chairman of the Security Commission, that such awards would make the law appear an ass. As Scott J. put it in December 1987, it would be part of the case for the 'absolute protection of the security services that .... could not be achieved this side of the Iron Curtain'; and perhaps since those words were spoken not even there.

In Parliament

The Bill was a faithful replica of the White Paper with one significant development concerning information relating to international relations. Although several minor amendments were made to the Bill in its Parliamentary passage, the government refused to cede ground on any of its major objectives.

The Home Secretary rejected accusations that only allowing six days on the floor of the House to debate all sixteen clauses of the Bill was 'niggardly'. Furthermore, the Committee stage was a Committee of the whole House. After a two and then a three line whip, the guillotine was imposed, an amendment to the Bill in Committee was not incorporated for consideration at Report stage, and inconsistent answers were given on crucial points. 'The effect of the guillotine was that, while some topics received thorough discussion, others were barely considered at all' (Winetrobe 1989). Indeed, Section 5, as we shall see, contains what could be a fatal flaw. In seeking to amend the Bill by introducing a public interest defence, Richard Shepherd reminded the Commons that, while Parliament might often pursue abuses of authority, it rarely raised them. In the Lords, Lord Hutchinson of Lullington, counsel in many OSA cases, challenged the government view that the reform was a liberalising measure. The six areas of information saw 'even greater restrictions' introduced, and in the past thirty years all prosecutions involving leaks to the media had involved the six areas. The statutory definitions of 'damaging' were wide and vacuous, with 'weak, inexact and unreliable' criteria, 'far removed from the central issue of the security of the state' (504 HL Debs, col. 1632, 9 March 1989).

And so it was that after seventy eight years, Section 2 had been reformed. Reform was, of course, needed. Of that there was no doubt. Section 2 had been used to bully and intimidate civil servants with some considerable effect on a number of different accounts. Now, the Government assured us, there was to be no more talk of catch-all provisions with well over 2,000 offences. The Act would target six specific areas. Civil service codes and statutes would be used to plug other gaps as we shall see. There would be no prosecution of those who had caused only embarrassment or distress to Ministers by their leaks; nor would pensions be stopped unless a conviction under the criminal law had been secured.[4] Let me now turn to the content of these so-called 'liberalising' measures.

The Official Secrets Act

The Act, which came into force on 1 March 1990, extends, with minor exceptions, to Northern Ireland and to offences committed abroad by

British citizens and Crown servants (Section 15). Prosecutions may only be brought with the consent of the Attorney-General or Lord Advocate, except for offences under Section 4(2). This safeguard has been claimed, on numerous occasions, to be more apparent than real, as the Attorney-General is, severally, protector of the public interest, lawyer, elected politician, member of the government, government legal adviser, and Crown, i.e. government, prosecutor. Given the judicial endorsement, *per* McCowan J., of the interests of the state as synonymous with the interests of the government of the day (*R v. Ponting*), it is hardly surprising that decisions of the Attorney-General have not infrequently been perceived as partial. Although Ministers may be consulted, 'the final decision is his alone' (Franks 1972: para. 37). In a different capacity, the Attorney-General was not consulted over the decision not to seek injunctions preventing publication of books containing revelations about MI5 and MI6 which were repeated in Spycatcher. In fact, the Attorney-General forced the Cabinet Secretary to retract a statement to the contrary which the latter had made in open court in New South Wales.

Authorised Disclosures

The distinction between an authorised and an unauthorised disclosure is central to the whole structure of the 1989 Act. The concept is also crucial for the operation of the Civil Service Pay and Conditions of Service Code. Some explanation is therefore required.

Throughout the 1980s it became evident to the government that the relationship between Ministers and civil servants was in need of reformulation. Civil servants had long abandoned the veil of anonymity with which their work was traditionally shrouded. A huge change in culture had taken place in the civil service brought about by the Financial Management Initiative and a significant reduction in manpower. There were other causes and effects. The role of civil servants in leaking the Solicitor-General's letter to Michael Heseltine in the Westland saga, the confusion into which the Ponting trial and acquittal threw the government, greater trade union activity and industrial unrest at GCHQ,[5] were all contributary factors. However, the deliberate placing of civil servants in the front-line of media and press attention by Ministers was not without importance. Furthermore, by the end of the decade, the wholesale devolution of managerial responsibility to executives and line managers running executive agencies outside the ministerial/departmental structure, and the attenuation of ministerial responsibility, all helped to place the minister/civil servant relationship under strain. The formal relationship was expressed in memoranda and Cabinet Office guidelines from Sir Robert Armstrong in 1985 and 1987 respectively. In these, he stated that civil servants were servants of the Crown. He added that the 'Crown' means, and is represented by, the government of the day whose ministers are answerable to Parliament. A civil servant's primary duty is to the minister in charge of the department in which they are serving and whom they must serve 'with complete integrity and to the best of their ability'. The maintenance of trust between ministers and civil servants, and the efficiency of government, required that the latter kept the confidences to which they become privy in their work (Armstrong 1985: 40-42).

Civil servants should not be requested to do anything unlawful, and nor should they knowingly and deliberately deny a person their legal rights (Civil Service Department 1979: 9). If legal advice confirms that action would be unlawful, a written report should be made to the permanent head of the department. When giving information to Parliament or the public, the overriding duty is to the minister. The minister controls all aspects of content, timing and manner of release. Ministers, for their part, owe a duty to give Parliament and the public as full information as possible about the policies, decisions, and actions of government, and not to mislead or deceive Parliament or the public (Cm. 9841). It is quite unacceptable for serving or former civil servants to seek to frustrate policies or decisions of ministers by the disclosure outside the government of information to which they have had access as a civil servant and which would be a breach of confidence.

I shall deal with civil service codes and disciplinary proceedings later. From the above, however, it is clear that the release of information operates under the authority of the minister. Ministers are, therefore, to a large extent, self-authorising; they do not leak, they brief. Senior civil servants are in substantially the same position (Franks 1972: para. 18; and Treasury and Civil Service Committee 1986: p.5), the extent to which they are self-authorising depending upon their position and seniority and what is necessary for the performance of their duties. Section 2 of the 1911 Act created an offence if Crown information was disclosed to someone 'other than a person to whom [the civil servant] is authorised to communicate it, or a person to whom it is in the interests of the state [the civil servant's] duty to communicate it'. The Act did 'not explain the meaning of the quoted words' (Franks 1972: para. 18). In *Ponting*, McCowan J. directed the jury that the 'interests of the State' were synonymous with the interests of the government of the day. He expressed no qualification. In so instructing, he wrenched from their context dicta of the Law Lords in

Chandler v. DPP ([1962] 3 All ER 142) which could be used to support Ponting's case where national security was not at stake.

At the root of the problem is an inherent conflict between the governing of a country by a particular government which may abuse its powers, and the idea of the state, or specifically the Crown, as representative of a larger collective weal which is bigger than any government. 'Those whose prime loyalty is to the government of the day look to the Crown as a more enduring expression of their position within the constitution (HC 92 II (1985-86): para. 3.2). The First Division Association of Civil Servants (FDA) has argued that loyalty to the Crown included the Crown in Parliament, thereby creating a special relationship between MPs and civil servants. The 'Crown in Parliament', however, is a legislative device, not an all pervasive constitutional relationship.

To avoid what must have seemed to any government as metaphysical meanderings, lawful authority for a disclosure by a Crown servant or government contractor under the 1989 Act means 'if, and only if, it is made in accordance with [an] official duty'. The established view would see an official duty emanating solely from within the official chain of command, going up to, and including the permanent secretary and minister as adviser to the Crown.

The 1989 Act provides that a disclosure by a government contractor is, tautologously, made with lawful authority if, and only if, it is made in accordance with an official authorisation, or for the purposes of the functions by virtue of which they are a government contractor without contravening an official restriction (Section 7(2)). Disclosure of protected information by any other person is made with lawful authority if, and only if, it is made:

(a) to a Crown servant for the purpose of his or her functions as such;
(b) in accordance with an official authorisation (Section 7(3));

The mysteries of self authorisation will remain. A party charged with an offence under Sections 1-6 of the 1989 Act may prove, with the onus on that party, that at the time of the alleged offence they believed that they had lawful authority to make the disclosure in question and had no reasonable cause to believe otherwise. Their simple belief is not enough, even if mistaken.

A recent order has prescribed certain persons as crown servants (S.I. 1990/200). Interestingly, the Comptroller and Auditor-General and the staff of the National Audit Office are included.

Security and Intelligence Information

Section 1 protects security and intelligence information, which is defined in subsection 9. The provision stipulates that members and former members of the services - MI5 and MI6 respectively - and 'notified' persons are guilty of an offence if without lawful authority they disclose any information, document or other article relating to security and intelligence acquired by virtue of their position as such a member/person. It is reasonable to suppose that MI5 and MI6 are not the only British security and intelligence services. Whether military intelligence is part of the security and intelligence services for these purposes is academic, as they would clearly be 'notified' if not (and see Section 1(9) OSA 1989). The Defence Committee has examined the activities of military intelligence, but the chair ruled out an investigation into MI5, arguing that the service was outside its jurisdiction.

In the Commons it was stated that 'carefully selected and mainly senior officials', as well as members of the armed services working in a 'few government departments' assessing intelligence information of the highest sensitivity and assisting Ministers, would be notified. Also proposed for notification would be those who work on providing the services with regular professional support for their operation and activities. These will usually be Crown servants. Members of the armed forces who undertake technical communications and work alongside the services in various parts of the world will be notified, as will Ministers and others 'with particular responsibilities or public duties in respect of the services' (145 HC Debs, cols. 1128-9, 25 January 1989). The government insisted that a notification would be secret, so no reasons would be given though, after denial and equivocation, it was accepted by the government that a notification would be judicially reviewable. Even with reasons, however, the possibility of a successful judicial review involving a matter of security and intelligence is extremely rare (*Council of Civil Service Unions v. Minister for Civil Service* [1985] AC 374; *R v. Secretary of State ex p. Ruddock; R v. Director GCHQ ex p. Hodges, The Independent* 21 July 1989). Notification will be in force for five years from the day on which it is served, though it may either be revoked within that period or indeed extended (Sections 1(8) and (6)).

Section 1(2) also covers statements purporting to be security or intelligence disclosures; i.e., vacuous 'big talk' or idle boasts by security and intelligence officers or former officers and notified persons. Unlike the common law, there is no defence for trivia, and no public interest defence. It is not true to suggest, therefore, with respect to the

Law Lords, that the OSA 1989 and the law of confidentiality are on a par (*Lord Advocate v. Scotsman* [1989] 2 All ER 852). Any disclosure within Section 1(1) and (2) under the 1989 Act is presumed damaging.

It is clear that the offences of aiding, abetting, inciting etc. in Section 7 OSA 1920 do not apply to the 1989 Act. But there are common law offences of aiding, abetting and incitement. If these offences were invoked by a prosecutor then it would add considerable uncertainty to the position of, e.g., a newspaper editor or publisher. The formless offence of conspiracy should also be kept in mind from the point of view of the recipient.

For Crown servants, other than members of the security services and notified persons, and for government contractors, both of which are defined in Section 12, an unauthorised disclosure is punishable as an offence if it is 'damaging'. By Section 1(4) a disclosure is deemed to be damaging if 'it causes damage to the work of, or any part of, the security and intelligence services'. No specific allowance is made for trivia or the public interest so that, for example, damage would be caused if a disclosure revealed that the service was engaged in murder (see Lord Donaldson MR [1988] 3 All ER 545 at 603-6, esp. 605 d-e). More sensationally, the government legislated via the back door for ministerial certificates to be introduced, in spite of their contrary claims. This was achieved as follows. Section 1(4) allows damage to be presumed where the disclosure is of information the unauthorised disclosure of which:

> would be likely to cause such damage [viz to security or intelligence] or which falls within a class or description of information, documents or articles the unauthorised disclosure of which would be likely to have that effect.

This will allow arguments to be 'less specific'. The prosecution will simply have to show that the information was classified under Section 1(4). Once that is established, the offence is made out. The classification will be that of a Minister and is evidence of its damaging quality, unlike the security classifications discussed above. Under Section 8(4) OSA 1920, the public and press may be excluded from a trial under the 1989 Act (Section 11(4)). Such an order excluding the press will prevent the public being informed of details.

Although the above provision has been described as an absolute offence, a defence is nonetheless available. The defence allowable under Section 1(5) involves the security or other relevant officer proving that at the time of the alleged offence they did not know, and had no reasonable cause to believe, that the information or documents related to security or intelligence. One might be tempted to think that they would have to be singularly unintelligent intelligence officers to plead ignorance successfully in this context. Where the offence is not absolute, non-notified Crown servants have to prove that they did not realise that the disclosure would be damaging.

In the case of recipients, such as newspaper editors, news media or publishers, Section 5 covers their unauthorised receipt and damaging disclosure of information, although I referred above to the danger of the use of common law offences of aiding and abetting offences under Section 1. 'Damaging' is established in the same way as for non-notified Crown servants under Section 1(4). However, the prosecution must prove in addition that the defendant made the disclosure knowing, or having reasonable cause to believe, that it is protected against disclosure under Section 1. In other words, *mens rea* has to be specifically established vis-a-vis the recipient's disclosure; it is not presumed as in the case of Crown servants. The relevant disclosure to the recipient will, under Section 5(1), be made by a Crown servant or government contractor without authority. Alternatively, it will be made after the servant or contractor has entrusted the information 'in confidence', either expressly or implicitly, and there was then an unauthorised disclosure. There are also offences covering situations where it was received by a third or fourth party and the disclosure to that party was made without authority by a person to whom it was entrusted 'in confidence'. A necessary condition for the offence is that the recipient is not committing an offence under Section 1-4 (which only cover Crown servants or government contractors). Section 5 creates the possibility of a chain *ad infinitum* from the perspective of recipients. However, mens rea (or a guilty intent) must be established in the case of each recipient and where the disclosure without lawful authority is by a government contractor or by a person to whom it was entrusted in confidence by a Crown servant or government contractor, the relevant disclosure must be by a British citizen, or it must take place in the UK, Channel Islands, Isle of Man or a colony. In other words a limitation to the territorial extent of the offence is introduced.

The government accepted that, as Section 5 only applies to disclosures by Crown servants or government contractors, former servants and contractors and their disclosures were not included. It should be noted that this shortcoming, from the government's perspective, is not remedied by Section 5(1) (a) (iii), which only covers a situation where an intermediary receives information in confidence. The government may be forced to use the civil law of confidentiality in such cases. This could be a substantial flaw in the 1989 Act, since it was aimed at circumstances similar to those at stake in the Peter Wright affair. Where a newspaper does not receive information from a person who received it in confidence, which would include a former security official, a prosecution under Section 5 may well flounder. And, it would not be possible to obtain an injunction under the civil law where a newspaper reported information received from a source not bound by confidentiality.

As a concluding comment on this section it has been well observed that when everything is secret, nothing is secret. The offence under Section 1 covering security officials seeks to achieve such total secrecy. It is a case of overkill and its very breadth may well prevent it meeting its objectives.

Defence

Section 2 of the OSA 1989 covers defence information and damaging disclosures by existing and former civil servants and defence contractors. The defendant can establish the defence that at the time of the alleged offence they did not know, and had no reasonable cause to believe, that the information related to defence or that its disclosure would be damaging. 'Damaging' is defined in Section 2(2). It is a disclosure which damages or is likely to damage the capability of the armed forces of the Crown, or any part of them, to carry out their tasks. It also covers a disclosure which leads to loss of life or injury to members of those forces, or to serious damage to the equipment or installation of those forces. Last of all, it covers those disclosures which otherwise endanger the interests of the UK abroad, seriously obstructs the promotion or protection by the UK of those interests, or endangers the safety of British citizens abroad.

There were fears that the section would include within its embrace disclosures about unnecessary wastage, inefficient production and sub-standard products, especially if these affected UK economic interests abroad. Section 2(4) defines 'defence', however, to include:

(a) the size, shape, organisation, logistics, order of battle, deployment, operations, state of readiness and training of the armed forces of the Crown;
(b) the weapons, stores or other equipment of those forces and the invention, development, production and operation of such equipment and research relating to it; [This would need to be a damaging disclosure, so the jury would be correct to consider factors which diminish the damage to UK military interests abroad by, for example, revealing extravagant waste.]

(c) defence policy and strategy and military planning and intelligence;

(d) plans and measures for the maintenance of essential supplies and services that are or would be needed in time of war.

For a party who is not a civil servant or a government contractor, Section 5 provides that their unauthorised receipt, or receipt in confidence, and subsequent unauthorised disclosure, is an offence where that person knows, or has reasonable cause to believe, that it is protected against disclosure by Section 2 and that it has come into that person's possession as under Section 5(1). The prosecution must establish *mens rea*, and that the disclosure was damaging, and that the defendant knew, or had reasonable cause to believe, that it would be damaging. Similar limits apply to a potential chain of recipients as applied in the discussion on the receipt of security and intelligence information.

This section would cover the notorious episode involving Duncan Sandys who used leaked information to reveal Britain's ill-prepared war defences prior to 1939. Apart from Parliamentary privilege for MPs, no defence would obtain to protect those who originally disclosed the information. The Sandys case prompted Sir Winston Churchill to denounce the use of the OSA to shield Ministers who have strong personal interests in concealing the truth about matters from the country.

International Relations

Section 3 is concerned with unauthorised disclosures of information relating to international relations by Crown servants and government contractors. Section 5 is concerned with the damaging disclosures of such information by others who have received the information within the terms of Section 5(1). For the former defendants, knowledge of the damaging nature of the disclosure will be presumed; for the latter it has to be proved. Offences under this section include the disclosure of information relating to international relations. It also covers 'any confidential information ... obtained from a State other than the United Kingdom or an international organisation, which is, or was, in the servant or contractor's possession by virtue of their position as such'. Section 3(5) defines international relations as relations between States, international organisations (IO), or between one or more States and one or more such organisations, and 'includes any matter relating to a State other than the United Kingdom or to an international organisation which is capable of affecting the relations of the United Kingdom with another State or with an international organisation.' IO would include the European Community (EC) and the UN, although Douglas Hurd expressed the view that the bulk of information from the EC was 'not confidential', and that most information received in confidence would fail the damage test (147 HC Debs, col. 429, 15 February 1989).

In spite of Mr. Hurd's assurance, if a journalist revealed information leaked by a civil servant that subsidies were being paid to companies purchasing privatised concerns which contravened EC law, then this would concern international relations and it may well be damaging to such relations. Or, once again, a disclosure which revealed Cabinet discussions and pejorative comments about the national characteristics of our EC partners and allies may be treated likewise. It could also cover the disclosure of information concerning inhumane treatment by an ally or trading partner of political opponents or minority groups. Where the broad test of 'damaging' is made out, the offence is established.

The test of damaging is to be found in Section 3(2). A disclosure damages, first, if it endangers the interests of the UK abroad, seriously obstructs the promotion or protection by the UK of those interests or endangers the safety of British citizens abroad, and secondly, if it is a disclosure of information which is such that its unauthorised disclosure would be likely to have any of those effects. The breadth of this latter category can be illustrated by an example. If a document was stamped 'confidential', or was obtained in circumstances making it reasonable for the state or international organisation to expect confidentiality, which is readily presumed in international relationships, then it will be treated as confidential for the purposes of the OSA, even if it would not be considered confidential under our civil law as judicially developed.

In the White Paper, it seemed that the government had created an absolute offence under this category. In fact, the Home Secretary and ministers were at pains to point out that the confidentiality or nature of documents might, but would not necessarily, be crucial (147 HC Debs, cols. 426-7, 15 February 1989). Even though otherwise innocuous information is stamped 'confidential', a jury may infer, but is not constrained to infer, that its unauthorised leak is damaging.

Crime

Existing and former Crown servants and government contractors are guilty of an offence where they make an unauthorised disclosure of information which is or has been in their possession because of their official position, and which results in one of the following:

(a) the commission of an offence. Events in Northern Ireland concerning security leaks of information on individuals have dramatically illustrated the sensitivity of information in the possession of the police and security forces, the disclosure of which has led to the murder of IRA suspects (Stevens: *The Times* 18 May 1990). The government has argued that the defence available in Section 4(4) (below) would protect disclosures about, for example, inefficient security systems;

(b) an escape from legal custody or the doing of any other act prejudicial to the safekeeping of persons in legal custody. One wonders about the situation where a prison officer reveals that a prison is at breaking point, or that inmates have been inhumanely treated and in consequence are on the point of insurrection;

(c) impeding the prevention or detection of offences or the apprehension or prosecution of suspected offenders (Section 4(2) (a)).

There is a general defence to these charges where the defendant can prove that at the time of the alleged offence they did not know and had no reasonable cause to believe that the disclosure would have any of those effects (Section 4(4)).

Furthermore, by Section 4(2)(b), unauthorised disclosures of information which are such that they are likely to have any of the above consequences are also an offence. A defendant may, however, show that they did not know, and had no reasonable cause to believe, that it was information to which the section applied (Section 4(5)); but note that this defence does not apply to Section 4(2)(b)).

It is important to appreciate that police records are not given blanket protection by the OSA, although police officers are prescribed as 'crown servants' for the purposes of the Act (Section 12). Where information is sold or disclosed, the law of corruption and disciplinary offences may have to be invoked against officers. It has been estimated that over one million people a year are vetted by employers with access to police records (*The Times* 8 May 1990) and the Home Affairs Select Committee has recommended a statutory body independent of the police to safeguard police records, many of which are currently out of date (Home Affairs Committee 1990).[6]

Where 'other persons', i.e. non civil servants and government contractors, receive information which is covered by the above provisions of Section 4, it is an offence when they make an unauthorised disclosure of information protected by Section 4 where they know, or have reasonable cause to believe, that it is protected against disclosure by Section 4(2). As in the other areas of information, the prosecution must prove, and cannot simply presume, the defendant's state of knowledge.

Information Relating to Special Investigation Powers

Section 4 also applies to any information obtained under 'special investigation powers'; viz. information which is obtained by warrant under the Interception of Communications Act 1985 and any related information, documents and articles, or obtained by warrant under the Security Service Act (SSA) 1989. Both Acts authorise what had hitherto been practised under the prerogative powers of national security and preservation of the peace (Birkett 1957). The powers of mail interception, and more latterly 'phone tapping', had always been assumed to exist, and that was felt to be sufficient justification until one Malone invoked Article Eight of the European Convention on Human Rights (ECHR) to challenge a telephone tap. The Court ruled that British practice was in contravention of the Convention in lacking an adequate legal basis (*Malone v. UK* (1984) 7 EHRR 14). Section 2 of the 1985 Act now allows letters to be opened and telephone conversations to be tapped under the warrant of the Secretary of State for specified reasons.

Interception without a warrant is a criminal offence. The Act establishes a Commissioner and a Tribunal to deal with complaints alleging abuses of warrant, though not interceptions carried out without a warrant, and sets out the criteria for issuing a warrant.

Section 3 of the SSA 1989 allows a warrant from the Secretary of State to authorise entry upon and interference with property, whether in the form of land or of personal possessions. Its most frequent use will be to authorise burglary and trespass, but 'interference' is not defined and will have the widest of ambits (cf. *Entinck v. Carrington* (1765) 19 St. Tr. 1030).

Section 4(3) OSA 1989 makes it an absolute offence for information, as described, obtained under the Acts to be disclosed without lawful authority by a Crown servant or government contractor. In fact, 'absolute' is not strictly accurate since a defendant can make out a defence similar to the one available for security and intelligence officers under Section 1 and described earlier.

Under Section 5, a person, for example a newspaper editor, who received information obtained under such warrants and who knowingly discloses it without authority, is guilty of an offence. The prosecution must prove that they knew or had reasonable cause to believe it belonged to such a category to establish a criminal offence. Actual knowledge of the nature of the information has to be proved. Once proved, and in most cases it will be glaringly obvious what its nature is, the offence will be made out no matter how trivial the information is and without reference to any public interest being served by its being made public. This is the strictest provision of all for third party recipients as no damage has to be proved.

The existence of this offence means that there would be no difficulty in prosecuting a Cathy Massiter, the former MI5 officer who revealed the targeting and intercepting of CND campaigners by the security service. This measure is particularly draconian and dangerous. It refuses to allow for the possibility that the rot is operating at such a high level that it is impossible to deal with it by internal devices. The investigatory and tribunal procedures under these two Acts, which seek to protect 'victims', are 'judicial-review proof'; that is to say that they cannot be reviewed by the courts. A revelation of a phone-tap without a warrant or other unauthorised invasion of privacy would not be covered by Section 4 OSA, but it may well be covered by Section 1 where perpetrated by security, intelligence or other notified officials.

Information Entrusted in Confidence to Other States

The government plugged a loop-hole by providing in Section 6 OSA 1989 that the unlawful disclosure of information relating to security, intelligence, defence or international relations which has been communicated in confidence by or on behalf of the UK to another State or IO, will be an offence if two conditions are satisfied. First, if it has come into the discloser's possession, whether originally disclosed to them or another, without the authority of the State or IO, or a member of the latter. Secondly, if the disclosure is not already an offence under the previous sections of the Act. Section 6 is aimed at punishing a disclosure of information which has been leaked abroad, even if already published abroad, without the authority of the State or IO to whom it was entrusted, or where the discloser otherwise has no authority. In other words, publishing a story in the UK which satisfies the above criteria and which is widely published abroad without authority, will constitute an offence. Publication with the authority of the state prior to disclosure is a defence.

The prosecution must prove that the defendant made a damaging disclosure knowing, or having reasonable cause to believe, that it is information as described in Section 6 and that its disclosure would be damaging.

Disclosure by Recipients Under Section 5

We have seen how receipt of information within the terms of Section 5, which is information protected by Sections 1-4, and its subsequent unauthorised disclosure by the recipient, will be an offence, and how a chain of offences may be committed. We also noted the limitations and exceptions concerning an unauthorised disclosure by a Crown servant or government contractor and those to whom such disclosures are made. We need only add that an offence is not committed where such a disclosure is made by a person who is not a British citizen or takes place outside the UK, the Channel Islands, the Isle of Man or a colony.

Finally Section 5 refers to Section 1 of the 1911 Act which concerns 'espionage' and which has already been discussed. Section 5 stipulates that it is an offence to disclose any information without lawful authority and which the discloser knows, or has reasonable cause to believe, came into his or her possession as a result of a contravention of Section 1 of the OSA 1911.

Safeguarding Information

Section 8 creates a variety of offences relating to the following. Crown servants (including a notified person under Section 1(1) who is not a Crown servant), or government contractors, commit an offence if they have in their possession information which it would be an offence under the Act to disclose without lawful authority and, being a Crown servant, they retain the document or article contrary to their official duty. A defence is available where they believe, and have no reasonable cause to believe otherwise, that at the relevant time they were acting in accordance with an official duty. Offences also cover the failure of a government contractor to comply with an official direction for the return or disposal of a relevant document, and the failure by a Crown servant or contractor to take such care to prevent the unauthorised disclosure of the document or article as a person in his or her position may reasonably be expected to take. This latter offence criminally punishes negligence.

Any person, including a past Crown servant or government contractor, who has information which it is an offence to disclose without lawful authority under Section 5, is guilty of an offence if they fail to comply with an official direction for the return or disposal of the information. Such persons are also guilty of an offence if they, in simple parlance, are negligent in looking after information entrusted to them in confidence by a Crown servant or contractor. A person is also guilty where they fail to comply with an official direction for the return of information protected by Section 6. Offences also cover disclosures which facilitate unauthorised access to protected information (Section 8(6)).

Miscellaneous Provisions

Offences under the Act are triable on indictment or summons, although some offences under Section 8 are triable by summons only. 'Trial by summons' means trial without a jury before magistrates who tend to be more sympathetic to the prosecution than juries and to be more conviction minded. The Act contains arrest and search provisions. By Section 11(4), the provisions of earlier secrecy legislation, allowing the public (including the press; see *In re Crook The Times* 13 November 1989) to be excluded from a trial on the grounds of national security, apply to offences under the 1989 Act, although there are minor exceptions under Section 8.

Under the Act, the term 'Crown servant' includes Ministers, civil servants, members of the armed forces, police officers and any other person employed or appointed in or for the purposes of any police force (*Lewis v. Cattle* [1938] 2 KB 454; *R v. Loat* [1985] Crim. L.R. 207). The Secretary of State may prescribe as Crown servants office-holders and some or all of their staff. The Comptroller and Auditor-General and employees of the National Audit Office have been so prescribed (S.I. 1990/200). Such orders are subject to the affirmative resolution procedure of the House of Commons (Section 12). The Secretary of State may also prescribe some or all of the members of staff of a range of bodies. 'Government contractor' is defined as a person other than a Crown servant who provides goods or services for the purposes of a Minister or body of Crown servants. The Act extends to Northern Ireland and to offences committed abroad by British citizens and, with minor exceptions, Crown servants.

The D Notice System

The Act is silent about the D Notice system. Any reference in the law to this 'system', which in the past has been a central feature in making the Official Secrets Acts workable, would have been a dramatic break with tradition.

However, the Defence, Press and Broadcasting Committee and the D Notice system are to survive, although the relationship between the press and media and government, whereby the former obtain information from the latter in return for not publishing material within a D Notice, was severely tested in the Spycatcher frenzy. Injunctions were obtained to restrain broadcasting of a programme about the security and intelligence services, even though the chairman of the committee had approved the material (*A-G v. BBC The Times* 18 December 1987). Along with the lobby system and its unattributable statements on behalf of the government, it represents a curious corporatist-like relationship, denoting a degree of self-regulation outside the law where principles can all too easily be compromised. Interestingly, the Commons Liaison Committee recommended in May 1990 a 'D Notice' system to halt leaks from select committees (HC 117 (1989-90); and see its report at HC 476 (1989-90)).

The OSA and the Question of Privilege

There are bound to be problems of considerable practical importance concerning the question of disclosures in contravention of the Act and privilege. The privileges in question are of two kinds. The first is that of an MP who cannot be prosecuted under the criminal law for statements made in the House or for those which are made in the course of Parliamentary proceedings. The second concerns the privilege between a lawyer and client and the giving of legal advice during which a disclosure of information protected by the 1989 Act is made.

The Act does not add to, or diminish, Parliamentary privilege. An MP will be protected as before, though the government resisted an attempt to allow a member of the public to be given immunity in passing protected information to an MP. The current position is that the privilege is that of the MP and no one else (see HC 173 (1937-8); HC 101 (1938-9)). Similarly, the 1989 Act does not affect the operation of the law relating to legal professional privilege, contrary to the views of the Law Society as represented by the Shadow Home Secretary (147 HC Debs, col. 503, 16 February 1989). Where, therefore, the disclosure is made with a view to obtaining legal advice on, e.g., whether it constitutes an offence, it is protected. It will not be protected where the disclosure was made to facilitate a crime to which the lawyer intended to be a party.

Civil Servants, Formalities, Confidentiality and the Disciplinary Code

The Official Secrets Acts which will still be signed at least twice in the life of every civil servant, are unlikely to be used as a basis for a prosecution where it can be brought under another provision concerning, for example, atomic installations, census information, VAT or one of eight categories of 'sensitive' information covered by legislation since 1987[7] (147 HC Debs, col. 1074, 22 February 1989). There are, however, crucial issues concerning civil servants' confidentiality and the disciplinary code which must be examined.

We have seen how events in the 1980s brought about a reformulated statement of the duties and responsibilities of civil servants to ministers. In an interesting commentary on his own statement concerning civil service loyalty, Sir Robert Armstrong described how new ministers had increasingly viewed civil service advisers with suspicion. They had often been regarded as unsupportive or even hostile, though Sir Robert did not associate himself with those sentiments (Armstrong 1985: 39). Mrs. Thatcher's administrations have been characterised by the use of special advisers from outside the civil service, most notoriously Sir Alan Walters, whose presence led to the resignation of Nigel Lawson in 1989. There was nothing new in such a practice: merely the extent of its use. Sir Robert reiterated his view that a 'non-political civil servant' must serve the government of the day 'with skill, energy and loyalty, whatever its complexion'. The 1985 note repeats that a duty of complete confidence is owed by the civil servant to the minister. A civil servant should not go public on account of a crisis of conscience, and the minister's instructions should be followed unless 'taking or abstaining from the action in question is felt to be directly contrary to a deeply held personal conviction on a fundamental issue of conscience' (Armstrong 1985: 41). Relevant information should not be withheld from a Minister. Where a conflict of loyalties occurs (and these 'will be very rare indeed' (ibid; p.43)), the civil servant should consult their superiors all the way to the Head of the Department and, if necessary, to the Head of the Home Civil Service. The First Division Association informed me that this procedure has not been used since its inauguration. Seemingly, about ten civil servants per annum are disciplined for breach of confidentiality or political bias. (159 HC Debs, col. 18, 30 October 1989). Interestingly, the Minister did not disclose the numbers of those disciplined for refusing to carry out work in breach of the guidelines which seek to prevent party political bias in the manner in which the government uses civil servants. The guidelines seek to prevent the abuse of civil servants by the government for party political purposes, for example the costing of an opposition's agenda or manifesto (Treasury and Civil Service Committee 1990). Sir Robin Butler, Armstrong's successor, did not accept the need for an independent tribunal to hear ethical complaints from civil servants and the Treasury and Civil Service Committee rejected a call from the First Division Association for an ombudsman to hear such complaints (Treasury and Civil Service Committee 1990).

One problem which has occupied the First Division Association concerns the fact that certain civil servants owe duties to others besides ministers. Tax inspectors must make an assessment according to law and owe duties of confidence, while lawyers for instance also owe professional obligations. Further, civil servants appearing before select committees are not empowered to obstruct the committees' investigations, although guidelines have been produced on subjects they may not discuss without referring the matter back to the ministerial head of the department. A select committee can also insist on the attendance of a named official, although questions are answered subject to the minister's instructions. However, the peculiar position of the Departmental Accounting Officer and the Public Accounts Committee (PAC) must be noted. The Accounting Officer must answer to the PAC for the proper expenditure of public monies. The Accounting Officer may also highlight the fact that a decision calling into question prudent and economic administration was that of the minister's personally.

On 1 March 1990, the new amendments to the Civil Service Pay and Conditions of Service Code came into effect. The relevant changes were necessitated by the OSA 1989. Paragraph 9911 states: 'All civil servants owe the Crown, as their employer, a duty of confidentiality' and confidential information must be protected 'whether or not the criminal law applies'. The duty of confidentiality continues after cessation of employment. Paragraph 9912 provides that where information is neither protected by the criminal law nor 'confidential', civil servants are expected to be prepared to make it available 'in accordance with Government policy and departmental instructions' and subject to paragraph 9913. This reminds civil servants of their duties of loyalty as well as confidentiality, of the need to check the scope of the criminal and civil law and the provision of information. There is also the duty to 'comply with any departmental instructions about the need to seek authority before taking part in activities which might involve the disclosure of official information or draw upon official experience', or to obtain advance clearance. Civil servants must not frustrate the policies or decisions of ministers by disclosures; must not make public statements which their departments might find 'objectionable' about individuals, including ministers, or organisations, whether public or private. Finally they must not take part in activities which might produce a conflict of interest. Punishment may include dismissal. This position may be contrasted with the Local Government and Housing Act 1989 which interestingly has provided a detailed legislative framework for the conduct of members and officers in local government. This is supplemented by regulations and a Government circular (Department of Environment Circ. 1990/8).

The Treasury and Civil Service Committee (1986: para. 6.9) have accepted that, while disclosures in the public interest do not justify criminal punishment, breaches of confidence still remain unprofessional and justify dismissal. An employee, including a civil servant, has no protection against the disciplinary consequences of a breach of confidentiality. The 'whistleblower' who reveals information, albeit in the public interest, has no protection in English law in such a case.

Such protection is provided in the USA where the Civil Service Reform Act 1978 allows officials to reveal information to the public which they reasonably believe to be in the public interest. Examples would include revelations of crime, corruption, gross waste, abuse of power, inefficiency, substantial public danger and so on. The law provides protection against reprisal. For certain sensitive posts such as at the FBI, or where security or intelligence information is concerned, the disclosure must be made to designated officials who inform the Congressional committees. The whistleblower is then informed of the outcome. Investigation of the allegation itself is by agency heads or by the Office of Inspector-General. 'Prosecution' of the employing agency takes place before the Merits Systems Protection Board and is carried out by the Office of Special Counsel. The Act provides a safeguard against administrative reprisal and punishment, though it does not provide a defence to a criminal prosecution. Following the Iran-Contra debacle, similar protection was promised for CIA officials.

In Canada, an interesting variation has incorporated the public interest defence to a breach of confidence, as developed by English law, into disciplinary proceedings involving Canadian civil servants at the federal level (*Fraser v. Public Service Staff Relations Board* (1985) 2 SCR 455). In England, the position is clear. There is no public interest defence to a disciplinary charge.

Where a former British security or intelligence officer or a civil servant wishes to publish memoirs using information acquired while in service then, leaving aside any question of copyright ([1988] 3 All ER at p. 567 and Copyright, Designs and Patents Act 1988), the official must obtain the permission of the head of their former department or even the Cabinet Secretary in order to avoid prosecution or injunctions. Interestingly, the arrangements covering CIA employees became a matter of wide comment during the Spycatcher episode. These allow former agents to agree to have proposed publications vetted prior to publication. However, the Supreme Court has decided that the CIA are entitled to the proceeds of sale, even where some disclosures are of non-confidential or unclassified information, an arrangement which does not deprive former agents of their First Amendment rights (*Snepp v. US* 444 US 507 (1980); *US v. Marchetti* 446 F 2d 1309 (1972)). The end result is that the public will not be prevented from knowing, but the absence of a financial reward will deter all but the publicly spirited. We shall see later how secrecy agreements are a pervasive practice in US federal employment.

As a concluding comment on the reform of Section 2, one can say that the 1989 Act is more restricted in its breadth and ambit than its predecessor. However, in the vital areas which it covers, the government has left no room for any other identification and protection of the public interest apart from its own. Whatever the self-denying ordinances adopted, the fact remains that the law allows, and provides no safeguard against, any government using the legislation in an unprincipled manner. For recipients, the provisions are unclear and will stifle publication and comment. Our only safeguard will be the House that passed the legislation, a 'perverse' jury, and Article Ten of the European Convention on Human Rights, the latter of which is not incorporated into our domestic law. (See p.52 below.)

The Security Service Act 1989

I have long taken the view that the information debate is about far more than the OSA and the operations of MI5 and MI6, as appears to be the attitude of Professor Griffith in recent writings (Griffith 1989). In Britain, where access to official information as a democratic right has rarely been high on the political agenda or a matter of significant interest to most members of the public, indifference has served the government well over the years. Allowing the democratic argument to be concentrated around the failings of official secrecy legislation and security rather than upon freedom of information or open government in its wider perspective obscures the larger issue. This larger issue was adverted to more than twenty years ago by the Fulton Report on the Civil Service when it claimed that there was too much secrecy in British government (Fulton 1968). It has received the official kiss of death for more than a decade.

Nevertheless, as I have written elsewhere (Birkinshaw 1988: ch. 1), the effort to extend some form of democratic control and accountability over the operations of those who protect our security and gather our intelligence, while maintaining appropriate levels of secrecy for their activities, provides a hotly contested arena. Here, the arguments of those who advocate maximum secrecy for security and intelligence, viz. the unqualified claims of the operatives, can be weighed against those who claim that the power wielded by such officials is too important to avoid any form of democratic accountability. To accept the debate in these latter terms and to give official sanction to such a debate would be to change the very nature of existing power configurations. The boundaries determining who is on the inside, and who the outside, of secrecy would be shifted irretrievably. For the British democrat, the image of so many East Europeans raiding the headquarters of security forces and rifling their files ranks with any moment in the tumultuous events of 1989 for its dramatic power. What information was being held on citizens in the nerve centre of unaccountable bureaucratic power? That question remains equally relevant in some of the old democracies of Western Europe.

The Security Service Act 1989 (SSA) puts MI5, the security service, on to a statutory basis. MI6,[8] the intelligence service, remains undisturbed by statutory oversight. Concentrating as the latter does on foreign intelligence (though with an active role in Northern Ireland affairs) its responsibilities fall more closely under the foreign affairs prerogative which has remained largely immune from Parliamentary regulation. The intrusions of MI5 into individuals' lives by way of surveillance, interception, bugging and burglary, however, was bound to be called into question. Furthermore, the use of the service by government departments, the BBC and the British Library for, *inter alia*, the vetting of job applicants, merely added to the clamour for regulation under statute, as opposed to an unsupervised prerogative of national security. For some time the Maxwell-Fyfe directive of 1952 provided the guidance under which the service operated. Enjoying no executive powers as such, MI5 operates in close liaison with Special Branch and regional crime squads. Like everyone else, its officials are formally subject to the law. However, any criminal liability would probably be protected by the exercise of the Attorney-General's prerogative not to prosecute as in the notorious 'Shoot to kill' policy in Northern Ireland (Stalker 1988), when officers of the RUC, apparently guilty of serious criminal offences, were not prosecuted in the 'public interest'. Much would depend upon the particular circumstances. No less a figure than Lord Donaldson, the Master of the Rolls, had expressed the view that the position of the service should be 'regularised' via Parliament (*A-G v. Guardian Newspapers* (No.2) [1988] 3 All ER 545 at 605). It was the threat of challenge, ultimately successful, via the Commission of Human Rights and the European Convention, which eventually prompted the British Government into legislative action (*H and H v. UK* App. No. 12175/86). The Commission and Court of Human Rights have given a wide leeway to the claims of national security and public safety in qualifying the protection of the Convention (*Leander v. Sweden* (1987) Series A No. 116; *Civil Service Union v. UK* (1988) 10 EHRR 269). However, they have both been critical of the enormous discretionary power of the executive to interfere with individuals' lives where the interference was not prescribed by law but merely by internal guidelines (*Malone v. United Kingdom* (1984) 7 EHRR 14).

In Lord Denning's report into the celebrated Profumo affair (Denning 1963), the Maxwell-Fyfe Directive was given extensive coverage, and it was the subject of detailed judicial analysis in the Spycatcher hearing before Scott J. Described as a 'part of the defence forces', MI5's duties were to defend the realm against attempts at espionage, sabotage or against actions or persons whether directed from within or without the country which may be judged to be subversive of the state. Their brief covers counter-subversion, although subversion itself is not defined in the Directive. Successive Home Secretaries have accepted the 1975 definition of Lord Harris, Minister of State at the Home Office:

> activities which threaten the safety or well-being of the State, and are intended to undermine or overthrow Parliamentary democracy by political, industrial or violent means (357 HL Debs, col.947, 26 February 1975).

There were numerous claims that this definition had been interpreted to allow surreptitious investigation and interference with perfectly legitimate (i.e. not otherwise unlawful under criminal or civil law) political and industrial activities, with no effective control over the subsequent use of the information acquired whether used in the private or public sectors. For an institution that was supposed to be 'absolutely free from political bias or influence', the definition was a red-rag to a bull, inviting individual members of the service to pursue their own political prejudices vis-a-vis trade unionists, especially when prompted by political overlords (Leigh and Lustgarten 1989). The Civil List and Secret Service Act 1782, only one of two statutes to name the service, provided that internal security measures were only to be directed against unlawful conspiracies, although the latter term had a far more extensive embrace in the eighteenth and nineteenth centuries.

Two further points should be addressed. From 1964, the Security Commission, which can only act on a reference from the Prime Minister, makes intermittent investigations into security lapses, and expurgated reports of its investigations are published. The chair is a Law Lord. There are internal Cabinet Office investigations prompted by the Prime Minister and civil service inquiries and select committees have floated around the periphery of security on a variety of occasions. In 1987, the Prime Minister appointed a staff counsellor to act as an internal ombudsman for those members of the two services who feel, in good conscience, a qualm about their work and instructions. This provides an internal grievance procedure which, the government hopes, will minimise the necessity for leaks.

The Legislation

The government accepted no amendments to the Security Service Bill. Like the OSA, the committee stage in the Commons was a Committee of the whole House.

Section 1 provides for the continuation of the Security Service under the Secretary of State. This would appear to indicate the potential authorisation of Secretaries of State other than the Home Secretary or Scottish or Northern Ireland Secretaries. From 1952, the Director-General of MI5 had been responsible to the Home Secretary, with a right of direct access to the Prime Minister. No reference is made to MI6 or to General Communications Headquarters. No provision is made for the use by the service of officers of the Special Branch or other forces. No reference is made to co-operation between British and overseas security and intelligence services, or to the use of 'private' contractors or agents.

The function of the Service 'shall be the protection of national security, and, in particular, its protection against threats from espionage, terrorism and sabotage, from the activities of agents of foreign powers and from actions intended to overthrow or undermine Parliamentary democracy by political, industrial or violent means' (Section 1(2)).

This leans substantially upon the erstwhile Harris definition. The Act contains provisions prescribing that the Service shall not take action to further the interests of any political party. However, all the weaknesses of the previous definition survive from the perspective of civil liberties, and there is nothing to prevent a prime minister condemning trade unions as the 'enemy within' as occurred in the miners' strike in 1984. Significantly, the Home Secretary in the debates on the Bill refused to define 'Parliamentary democracy'. As Leigh and Lustgarten express it:

> It is easy to imagine many in the Service, and indeed many Ministers, treating "Parliamentary democracy" as the subjects' right to vote once every few years and their obligation to obey the rest of the time. Civil disobedience therefore becomes subversion. This unsatisfactory state of affairs is compounded by the reference to "undermining", which imparts no limitation of immediacy or directness. (Leigh and Lustgarten 1989: 807)

The Act contains no explicit safeguards against improper instructions from Ministers, apart from those of a party political nature, although the role of the staff counsellor for officials should be recalled. The 1952 Directive authorised non-compliance with ministerial requests requiring a 'misuse' of the Service. In Australia, where the Attorney-General instructs an inquiry to commence or discontinue in circumstances where the Director-General feels that the instruction is improper, the instruction has to be in writing and copies have to be sent to the Prime Minister and the Inspector-General who oversees the Service and deals with complaints. In the case of political misuse, the matter has to go on record.

A further function of the Security service is to safeguard the economic well-being of the UK against threats posed by the actions or intentions of persons outside the British Islands. Given the Act's intention, this would cover the activities of MI5 within the UK as, for example, in relation to operations through OPEC member states' embassies in London.

Under Section 2, a Director-General continues to control the Service, albeit now with statutory recognition. The Director-General, who is appointed by the Secretary of State, is responsible for the efficiency of the Service and for ensuring that there are arrangements for securing that no information is obtained by the service except that which is necessary for the proper discharge of its functions. The Director-General is also to ensure that no information is disclosed by the service except so far as is necessary for like purpose or to prevent or detect serious crime. One wonders how effective this safeguard will be given the report of the Home Affairs Committee which was extremely critical of the records kept by police forces which gave information on well in excess of 500,000 individuals to departments, agencies and local authorities in 1989. It described as 'ill-defined' the power which police forces possess to give information to private employers. It also found serious inaccuracies in the information produced, and the Committee recommended a statutory, independent, agency to replace the National Identification Bureau (Home Affairs Committee 1990). It is important to note that the Director-General himself is charged with ensuring the party political neutrality of the activities of the Service.

Safeguarding of Information Held By The Service

To safeguard information held by the Service, which includes in the region of one million individual files, provisions will be approved by the Secretary of State allowing disclosure of personal information for use in determining whether a person should be employed, or continue to be employed, by any person, or in any office or capacity (Section 2(3)). This covers the use of such information for vetting purposes. The provisions need not be published. The Director-General reports annually on the work of the Service to the Prime Minister and Secretary of State, and may make additional reports to either of them on any matter relating to its work. Mrs. Thatcher has claimed that she has been too forthcoming to Parliament with security information. Given the Spycatcher episode and the running sore of the 'dirty tricks' revelations and worse from Colin Wallace,[9] as well as serious security breaches, she could not have avoided Parliamentary statements. But she has answered Parliamentary Questions on the Service: matters which are generally out of order in the House and exclusively under executive control. The Prime Minister keeps informed on security and intelligence matters via the Security Co-Ordinator and Joint Intelligence Committee in the Cabinet Office, and the Cabinet Secretary. The Prime Minister, rather than the Home Secretary, makes statements about the Service, if indeed they are made at all.

The Security Commissioner

Under Section 4, the Prime Minister appoints the Security Commissioner who is a person who holds or who has held high judicial office. The Commissioner has to keep under review the exercise by the Secretary of State of his powers under Section 3. This latter section empowers the Secretary of State to authorise entry upon or interference with property by warrant. Such warrants may be issued where they are necessary to obtain information which is likely to be of substantial value in assisting the Service to discharge any of its functions and which cannot reasonably be obtained by other means. The Secretary of State must be satisfied that adequate arrangements exist covering the disclosure of such information. A warrant lasts for six months from the day on which it was issued. Unlike the Police and Criminal Evidence Act 1984, no information is privileged against such a security warrant. Information covered by legal professional privilege (see above p.31) would, however, be inadmissible in court. With all respect to Lord Camden's famous words from *Entick v. Carrington* ((1765) 19 St.Tr. 1030) that 'it is the law and it is in the books', statute has allowed the executive to do what the common law prohibited (cf. *R v. IRC ex p. Rossminster* [1980] AC 952).

The Commissioner has a right of access to all information and documents in the possession of every member of the service and every official in the Secretary of State's department. The Commissioner reports to the Prime Minister annually and may report at any time on any matter relating to the discharge of those functions. The Prime

Minister has to lay a copy of the annual report before each House, but may exclude any item from the report the publication of which 'would be prejudicial to the continued discharge of the functions of the Service'. The Commissioner has to be consulted about the exclusion (Section 4(7)), and a statement on any exclusion is included in the report to Parliament.

Modern technology has ensured that telephone interceptions, for instance, can easily occur without the remnant of any physical evidence. Given the complexity of information technology, the presence of the Commissioner can all too easily be by-passed, even when the Commissioner is operating with the best will in the world and with appropriate vigilance.

Complaints

Complaints about the inquiries or activities of the service may be made to the tribunal, consisting of between three and five lawyers (Section 5). Basically 'any person' may complain to the Tribunal if they are aggrieved 'by anything' which they believe the Service has done in relation to them or their property. The complaint is to be investigated in accordance with Schedule 1 of the Act unless the tribunal considers that the complaint is vexatious or frivolous. Considering the obvious difficulty a complainant will have in obtaining relevant information, such a barrier becomes much more formidable than might appear at first sight. The tribunal must investigate whether the service has conducted inquiries in relation to the complainant, and whether the inquiries had ceased or were continuing at the time the complaint was made. It is also instructed to inquire whether the service had reasonable grounds for investigating the complaint in the discharge of its duties. Where inquiries are being made about the complainant on the grounds of membership of a category (e.g. Greenpeace, CND, TUC, National Front) regarded by the service as requiring investigation, the service's belief in that person's membership of the category shall be regarded as reasonable grounds for making inquiries. The tribunal may refer to the Commissioner any case where they believe investigation of members of a category is not justified. They may also determine whether the service had reasonable grounds for believing information disclosed for employment purposes was true.

Property complaints, which include those relating to any place where a complainant resides or works, are to be referred to the Commissioner who investigates whether a warrant has been issued under Section 3 (Sched. 1 para. 4). The Commissioner may only investigate complaints where a warrant has been issued and relating to whether the Secretary of State was acting properly in issuing or renewing it. In making this determination, the Commissioner applies the principles of law applicable by a court on judicial review (*R v. Secretary of State for the Home Department ex p. Ruddock*). The tribunal must be informed of the decision.

Unauthorised interference is a matter for the criminal or civil law rather than the Commissioner, although the tribunal may refer to him any case investigated by them where, in spite of a negative conclusion:

> it appears to the Tribunal from the allegations ... that it is appropriate for there to be an investigation into whether the Service has in any other respect acted unreasonably in relation to the complainant or his property (Sched. 1 para. 7(2)).

It is not entirely clear whether this would include a property complaint where there was an interference by the service without a warrant. In relation to such a complaint, rather than investigating it itself, the tribunal refers the matter to the Commissioner (Sched. 1 para. 1). The latter cannot deal with a case where there is no warrant, but the Commissioner's conclusion in such a case, albeit negative, is given to the Tribunal, and through it to the complainant. The Interception of Communications Act 1985 does not allow for the investigation of complaints about unauthorised taps or intercepts and the exclusion of such complaints was probably also the intention of the proponents of the SSA. However, it is a serious shortcoming if the SSA excludes such complaints and the spirit of Schedule 1 para. 7 seems capable of including them, although such an interpretation would be seen in some quarters as strained. Para. 7(3) allows the Commissioner to report any matter referred to him under the paragraph to the Secretary of State, who, as well as taking such action as he feels fit, may also provide the remedies available to the tribunal under para. 6. But it remains the Secretary of State's decision. Remedies include the cessation of inquiries and destruction of records, compensation, and quashing of warrants.

The tribunal may demand from members of the service such information as they require for their statutory functions, though this does not extend to other government officials. Decisions of the tribunal and the commission under Schedule 1 are expressed not to be subject to appeal or to be questionable in any court of law (Section 5(4)). In all the circumstances, the courts are unlikely to exercise their ingenuity to undermine this provision and allow judicial review (cf. *Anisminic v. FCC* [1969] 1 All ER 208). Crucially, the tribunal does not have to give reasons for decisions, and they must not disclose any information or documents without the consent of the donor. Many such donors will be covered by Section 1 OSA 1989.

The Absence of Parliamentary Oversight

The 1989 Act leaves a great deal to be covered by custom and practice. This fact is projected into prominence when security legislation from overseas is examined. The working relationship of the Prime Minister with the Service is not explained and no reference is made to direct access to the Prime Minister by the Director-General as in the 1952 Directive. The statute only deals with reports by the Director-General. Nor does the statute dwell on the amount of information given to the Secretary of State or the independence of the Director-General from ministers, in spite of the restrictions on party political grounds.

Most importantly, the Act does not provide for any real form of Parliamentary oversight if we disregard the censored reports which it receives. At one time, information on the service was subject to an absolute prohibition, but more recently some limited information has emerged during debate and in answers to Parliamentary questions (see, e.g. Cm. 8787). Even so, information has been exceedingly exiguous and specific questions on the subject are normally likely to be ruled out of order. Questions mentioning the security or intelligence services are usually allowed, providing they do not seek information about individuals or operations (Committee of Privileges HC 365 (1986-87): paras 37-39 and Annex D). The Comptroller and Auditor-General does not audit the service in spite of the fact that a former Auditor-General, Sir Gordon Downey, believed that he should. Equally important is the fact that the Public Accounts Committee has no role in relation to its expenditure. Several select committee reports have touched upon security and related themes and the Defence Committee decided to investigate the events surrounding Colin Wallace's accusations insofar as they related to the Ministry of Defence and to maladministration in general.

From a constitutional point of view, one of the most glaring omissions is the absence of a precise statutory code of the powers of the service. The government would argue, of course, that such a code would inhibit the effectiveness of the service. Such knee-jerk responses might be less objectionable if adequate grievance procedures existed. Current procedures are uncertain in their scope, and do not cover complaints about activities before 18 December 1989 unless inquiries were continuing at that date. In any event, the 'system' - by which I mean the service and all those within and without the service who serve or assist it - is likely to seize up if there is unlawful action in contravention of, or without, a warrant or against the guidelines and an injured victim wishes to sue. Where the source of information to a third party is a security official, the latter will probably be prosecuted under Section 1 OSA 1989 for the disclosure. It is unlikely that the tribunal will keep the identity of such an official confidential from government. It is interesting to compare this with the government's decision to allow security officials to give evidence behind a screen at the inquest into events leading to the deaths of three terrorists in Gibraltar in 1988.

What is also controversial and of importance constitutionally is the fact that it is not even clear whether the Act, vague as its essential provisions are, is the exclusive source of authority and power of the Service. In *R v. Home Secretary ex p. Northumbria Police Authority* ([1988] 1 All ER 556) the Court of Appeal accepted that a prerogative power, in this case 'maintaining the peace', could survive a statutory enactment covering the same subject area. Traditional doctrine has it that where a statute is passed on a subject hitherto under the prerogative, the statute takes precedence unless Parliament indicates the contrary intention. In *Northumbria*, the court held, albeit *obiter*, that in order to exclude the prerogative, Parliament must intend the legislation to create a monopoly of power, either expressly or by necessary implication. There was no such intention, the court held, behind the Police Act 1964. Were this to apply in the present context then an ancient prerogative would be rattling its chains once more down the centuries.

There are numerous ways in which officialdom can ruin a person's life besides imprisoning or tortiously or criminally injuring him, yet the total package of security legislation hardly constitutes a constitutional code. The *Northumbria* decision renders uncertain the extent of the service's authority. Mr Hurd insisted that the government 'are taking an area of public policy out of the realm of the prerogative and putting it into the realm of statute' (145 HC Debs, col. 213, 7 January 1989). This is an over-sanguine view.

Oversight of Canadian and Australian Security and Intelligence Services
During the passage of the Bill through Parliament, opponents from all parties emphasised frequently the far more detailed legal regulation of the Canadian and Australian Security and Intelligence Services. The relevant Australian legislation, the Australian Security and Intelligence Organisation (ASIO) Act 1979, as amended, is fifty six pages long. The British SSA is only eight. The ASIO contains detailed provisions on the organisation and its Director-General, sets out the functions and powers of the organisation and provides for legal assistance for complainants, costs, witnesses' fees etc. before the

Security Appeals Tribunal which deals with security clearance. The Inspector-General of Intelligence and Security acts as an ombudsman for the public and has unlimited powers to obtain information. An agreed report may be made to a complainant. All ministerial directions on security and intelligence must be shown to the Inspector-General.

The Act also provides for a Parliamentary Joint Committee on the Australian Security Intelligence Organisation, though its remit is limited. It cannot review foreign intelligence material or 'operationally sensitive' matters relating to the collection of information and it cannot originate inquiries into individual complaints concerning the activities of the organisation. The Committee nevertheless possesses wide powers to obtain information, although a ministerial certificate may bar the giving of evidence or production of information. Copies of the certificate have to be given to the President of the Senate and to the Speaker of the House.

The Canadian Security Intelligence Act 1984 (see McDonald 1981), the operation of which is to be reviewed by both Houses or the House of Commons by 1990, defines the tasks of the Service. In addition to security clearance, Section 12 of the Act stipulates that the Service:

> shall collect, by investigation or otherwise, to the extent that it is strictly necessary ... information and intelligence respecting activities that may on reasonable grounds be suspected of constituting threats to the security of Canada, and, in relation thereto, shall report to and advise the government of Canada.

Warrants are also subject to judicial control. An Inspector-General of the Services is entitled to any information under the control of the Services relating to the Inspector-General's duties. However, confidences of the Queen's Privy Council for Canada are excluded. Reports from the Director of the Service go to the Minister and Inspector-General, the latter of whom reports to the Solicitor-General and the Security Intelligence Review Committee (SIRC). The SIRC is comprised of Privy Councillors who are not members of Senate or the House of Commons and who are appointed by the Governor in Council. It has the general duty of reviewing the performance by the Service of its duties and functions. This includes acting on Ministerial directions. It also investigates complaints from anyone about anything done by the Service unless it is trivial, or unless a satisfactory response has already been given or another statutory remedy is available. The procedure is specified in the statute, whereas the SSA Tribunal in Britain is master of its own. The SIRC reports to the Minister, the Director and the complainant with its recommendations.

An attempt to introduce a Security Service Review Committee consisting of five Privy Councillors was rejected by the Government in debates on the Bill for the UK, as was an amendment for a Parliamentary Select Committee on Security. Such a committee, said Mr. Hurd, would be an *alter ego* of the security service itself (145 HC Debs, cols. 106-7, 16 January 1989). 'Too many spooks spoil ...' Parliamentary oversight would undermine its efficacy. No explanation was forthcoming as to why Commonwealth experience was unsuitable for the British system of government.

In the debates on the British Bill, Mr Rupert Allason MP remarked that less information is now available on interceptions than before the 1985 Interception of Communications Act came into effect. To ensure a supply of information from the Service on its activities, Richard Shepherd MP tabled an amendment requiring it to publish at ten yearly intervals from 1999 onwards details of some of its major activities. The details would include interception warrants, numbers of complaints referred to the tribunal, numbers of positive vetting referrals handled, an account of the Service's opinion on current threats and priorities, a case history relevant to the Service's work from each branch, and a statement of the Director-General relating to any significant changes in practice (HC Debs col. 245, 16 January 1989). The amendment was rejected.

One final comment sums up the dilemma of leaving control and accountability within too narrowly confined parameters in this secret world. It came from Michael Mates MP, Chairman of the Defence Committee and stalwart supporter of official secrecy, when speaking of the allegations of Colin Wallace. There was, he argued, no clear evidence of a cover up, and until there was the need for an inquiry was not made out!

The OSA and SSA of 1989 are, on balance, marginal improvements on the pre-existing position in the secret state. The breadth of the former Section 2 has been narrowed and there has been a limited legal regulation of one part of the secret organs of the State. Yet it must be said that this is small beer in the overall scheme of things.

Let me now broaden our inquiry to address not merely the maintenance of secrecy but the position concerning the whole information debate in contemporary Britain. There are numerous developments taking place, but they tend to be unprincipled and unsystematic. I will argue that a necessary development is coherent legislation providing for freedom of information in central government.

The Information Debate

So far the discussion has concentrated upon the maintenance of secrecy and the steps taken by the British government to ensure an appropriate cloak and mask over its operations. However, we live in a world which is being forever compressed by the advance of information technology. We are bombarded by information from media, press and advertising agencies, the reliability of which we can frequently only guess at. Information has become, in contemporary language, mega-business. The 'reforms' in our secrecy laws have a curiously dated quality when set in the context of the information debate currently preoccupying much of the Eastern as well as Western world. It is pertinent to highlight the fact, therefore, that one of the themes running through much legislation in the 1980s has, ironically, given our discussion so far, been access to information. Unfortunately, this has not yet extended to central government. In 1985 the government announced that it was prepared to listen to arguments in favour of open government and access to information, and to respond to each case on its merits. Some legislation, such as the Data Protection Act 1984, which opened up personal computerised records to data subjects, was forced upon the government by international obligations. The Local Government (Access To Information) Act 1985 has been extended beyond local government and, like the Access To Personal Files Act 1987, the Access to Medical Reports Act 1988, and the Environment and Safety Information Act 1988, it started life as a Private Member's Bill, as indeed did the Access To Health Records Act of 1990. To guarantee their passage through Parliament, the proponents had to accept government amendments of their Bills which, inevitably, and significantly, weakened the force of the original version.

The Local Government (Access To Information) Act is a remarkable statute, as yet little used, which not only allows access to documents, reports and background papers to reports, but also provides access to the meetings of councils. This includes committees and sub-committees, but excludes working parties which are not committees (*R v. Eden DC ex p. Moffat The Times* 24 November 1988). The Local Government and Housing Act 1989 also enacts various recommendations from reports (Widdicombe 1986; Department of the Environment 1988) addressing the need for greater legal regulation of local authority administration to reduce the perceived problem of abuse of control by dominant political groupings. These abuses manifested themselves in restricting the flow of information, the establishment of single party committees, political appointments, the use of political advisers and the absence of suitable declarations of interests by local authority members (Birkinshaw 1990). The Act followed detailed legal regulation of local authority publicity. This spate of regulation over the conduct of local government is in stark contrast to the absence of such regulation in central government administration. This is the more worrying given the introduction of a computerised government data network, the ease with which information may be transferred between departments, and the ever increasing sophistication of information technology. In his report for 1989-90, the Data Protection Registrar highlighted the growing use of identifying numbers encoding personal information, thereby facilitating the process of computer-matching; i.e. running a number through a series of computers (HC 472 1989-90). He also observed that complaints to his office from data subjects had more than trebled from the previous year.

That the British constitution runs on conventions rather than statute is one of those shibboleths learned, rarely understood and soon forgotten by students of the British constitution. The Westland episode of 1986 revealed simultaneously the fog with which the doctrine of ministerial responsibility envelopes the working of government, and the extent to which the doctrine has broken down as an effective legitimating device. The doctrine was invoked to prevent civil servants appearing before a select committee investigation into the events surrounding the leaking of the Solicitor-General's letter to the then Defence Secretary Michael Heseltine. The Trade Secretary, Leon Brittan, saw fit to break the anonymity in attempting to protect his own position (Birkinshaw 1988: ch. 4).

A further and substantial inroad into the doctrine of ministerial responsibility is contained in the government's 'Next Steps Initiative' whereby executive agencies will assume responsibility for areas of administration from departments of state. Responsibility for performance will be devolved down the line to chief executives and line managers to achieve set targets, objectives and budgets. As yet, there has been little evidence of original constitutional thinking to accompany the innovatory force of the developments. The means of establishing agencies is normally by 'framework documents' rather than statutes. So far these have all been published. But compare that with the provisions of the US Freedom of Information Act and the publicly available information on the organisation of executive departments and regulatory agencies discussed below. When the second permanent secretary at the Cabinet Office gave evidence to the Treasury and the Civil Service Committee on the initiative, he stated that he did not believe it desirable to introduce legislation to change accountability on an overall basis. At present the monitoring of agencies by departments in the UK is to a great extent a well-kept secret.

In any discussion on the information debate one has to address the role of Parliament, particularly its ability to extract information from the Government and to inform the public (Frankel 1990). Political commentators have observed that the advent of TV into the Chamber has not only served to raise the latter's profile but to increase the desire of Ministers to make statements there, rather than through press releases. Be that as it may, the most important weapon available to the Commons is the select committee system. Even so the treatment of committees by ministers and ex-ministers has all too frequently been cavalier. The government's antagonism to Parliament playing anything more than a rubber stamping role in matters of real import was evident in its exclusion of Parliament from any role of oversight in the SSA, its thwarting of Parliament's attempt to reform the OSA and the attempt to prevent MPs viewing the Zircon satellite film in the confines of the House by injunction (HC 365 1986-7). The problem is one relating to the relationship between government and Parliament and the powerlessness of the latter except in rare fits of outrage. It is trite but true to remark that Parliamentary supremacy means governmental supremacy as long as the latter's majority is intact. The ability of MPs to obtain information in select committees, circumscribed as that is by civil service guidelines, ultimately depends upon party political will. Strong government is viewed as being incompatible with accountable government. Whatever devolutionary or decentralising trends might ultimately emerge in our government structure, the ability of select committees to obtain information must depend upon a surer basis than a vote of the whole House exercised on party political lines.

I pause to make brief comment only about the devolvement of governmental responsibilities on to the private sector, the off-loading of public responsibilities, privatisation and the increasing public/private interface in the delivery of essential services and in the generation of wealth and enterprise. Quite starkly, such developments are rarely accompanied by any appropriate accountability mechanisms and display the worst features of secrecy in the tradition of British government. The sale of Rover plc to British Aerospace and the use of illegal 'sweeteners' by the Department of Trade and Industry to secure the sale is but one, albeit one quite dramatic example. Colleagues and I have shown elsewhere how fatal to constitutionalism and democracy itself these developments are in the dual absence of a concept of the public realm and the public interest that is not blinded by nineteenth century mythology and the lack of freedom of information (Birkinshaw et al 1990).

The Courts

Without an equivalent to a First Amendment, constitutionally guaranteeing freedom of speech, it is far less likely that the courts are going to be centre-stage in the arbitration of disputes concerning an informed public and *raison d'etat* in an arena which is not heavily weighted in favour of the latter. At present, in addition to a process of judicial review which is uncertain and often disappointing in its scope, the arbitration takes place as an item which is incidental to consideration of the extent and scope of ordinary torts, such as confidentiality, albeit adapted to application in a governmental context. In certain areas, especially national security, the courts have abjured any pretence of oversight, subject only to the executive providing some evidence that national security is involved. What was also remarkable and very worrying in the Spycatcher case was the sight of so many senior judges jockeying to be more executive-minded than the executive in their efforts to suppress what was publicly available. In the free world, whose boundaries are ever shifting, the actions of the Court of Appeal and House of Lords in the interlocutory proceedings in allowing 'prior restraint' of the publication by newspapers of news items on Spycatcher caused bewilderment. First of all, because the courts were attempting to achieve the impossible: the cat, the horse or whatever had bolted. Secondly, in that the matter had not been satisfactorily resolved by the government long before it became a public issue in the courts. Whether through inappropriate use of the law of contract, the issue of a pension, or selective suppression of information, the government had continually allowed itself to be wrong-footed. The majority of Law Lords revealed themselves in a repressive, even ugly mood in restraining the press. Lords Bridge and Oliver, in dissenting, both expressed their concern at the majority's reasoning. Lord Bridge claimed that for the first time in his legal career he was left with a revelation of the void in our law when it comes to the protection of civil liberties (*A-G v. Guardian* [1987] 3 All ER at 346; cf. his Lordship in *Hector v. A-G of Antigua and Barbuda* [1990] 2 All ER 103 (PC)).

In the proceedings for a permanent injunction against the newspapers, Scott J. delivered a judgment which portrayed judicial decision-making at its best in its grasp of legal principle and its concern over the exaggerated claims of an unbridled executive. The important points from his judgment we examined above. Nevertheless, the approach of the Law Lords at the interlocutory stage is likely to be influential with judges in future public secrets cases involving confidentiality and prior restraint applications. Certainly, the courts have been restrictive in curbing press and media freedom by the use of the law of contempt. The Court of Appeal, for instance, banned nightly dramatised re-enactments by TV of public proceedings in the court during the day as this might adversely affect 'the public view of the judgment' (*In re Channel Four TV Co. Ltd. The Times* 18 December 1987). The same court has ruled that exclusion of the public from judicial proceedings in a criminal case included the exclusion of the press, something which was contrary to established practice (*In re Crook The Times* 13 November 1989). The Spycatcher saga left another unfortunate precedent for the press and media in that publication of information in the book by papers not enjoined in the original injunction was also held to be punishable as a contempt (*A-G v. Newspaper Publishing PLC* [1988] Ch. 333; *In re A-G v. The Observer Ltd The Times* 9 May 1989; see *The Times* 28 February 1990; and n.b. *Re Lonhro* [1989] 2 All ER 1100).

One further inhibition concerned the interpretation of Section 10, Contempt of Court Act 1981. This allows a person responsible for a publication, including a broadcast, to protect sources of information protected from disclosure, unless disclosure, which remains a matter for the court's discretion, is necessary for one of four reasons including being 'in the interests of justice'. Unpersuaded by dicta of Lord Diplock, the Court of Appeal and House of Lords held that 'in the interests of justice' was not confined to the due administration of justice or the proper resolution of an issue before the court. It included the right to pursue an action. How speculative that right may be, for example, for a breach of confidentiality, is not clear (*X Ltd v. Morgan Grampian (Publishers) Ltd* [1990] 2 All ER 1). It is right and proper that the courts fulfil their obligations to protect our rights, including those to confidentiality. But those protections can all too easily be used as a muzzle. It is true that the judges emphasised the importance of the free-flow of information and that the discretionary nature of the power to order disclosure only arises after necessity has been established by the plaintiff in a manner appropriate to the context of the claim. The courts will also consider a wide variety of factors including the manner in which the information was originally obtained and the public importance of disclosing the information from the source when balancing competing claims. However, the decision has sent a shock-wave through the quality press whose journalists are bound by their own code to maintain the confidentiality of sources.

The decision comes at a time when the use of legal restraints on broadcasting and the media have increased, including the overt banning by the Secretary of State of sound broadcasts by members of prescribed organisations. Political interference has been seen to have become more strident in cases such as Real Lives, concerning Northern Ireland terrorists, and Death on the Rock, a programme about the shooting of IRA terrorists in Gibraltar (Bolton 1990). There is an increasing risk of financial hegemony becoming established as fewer and fewer owners of national newspapers dictate the tone and content of the subject matter. An emasculated BBC and commercial franchises auctioned to the highest bidder may not be as likely now as they were when the broadcasting White Paper was published (Home Office 1988). But our law is too weak in too many areas of the media to prevent the public interest being equated with the free-play of market forces and the depth of a particular pocket.

The growing familiarity of, indeed attraction for, the European Convention of Human Rights by many of our senior judges was put in context when the Court of Appeal was asked to review directives by the Home Secretary banning broadcasts by members of prescribed organisations (effectively terrorist groups and their political associations in Northern Ireland). The Convention is not part of our domestic law, but it has to be used as an aid to the interpretation of unclear or inconsistent legislation and the common law. The court held it could not invoke Article 10 of the Convention guaranteeing freedom of expression and information when construing statutory regulations or orders which were allegedly vague, as it could in interpreting a statute with those defects. The statute in question was clear and unambiguous and the Convention could not be prayed in aid (*R v. Secretary of State Home Dept. ex p. Brind* [1990] 1 All ER 469). It therefore expressed the inviolable will of Parliament. This blunt approach, however, does not address the crucial issue of whether the discretion to ban must be subject to an implied limitation to be exercised in accordance with the Convention (Jowell 1990: 153). The statutory power to ban must be exercised reasonably, but the Court held that there was no discrete doctrine of proportionality in English law. Proportionality, in this context, means that governmental objectives must not be pursued by excessive or unnecessarily heavy-handed means. Proportionality was instead subsumed within recognised heads of judicial review, such as perversity or abuse of power or irrationality, which usually require evidence of manifest, if not dramatic wrong doing rather than heavy-handed or excessive exercise of a dominant executive power. Nor was there a breach of the duty in Section 4 (1) of the Broadcasting Act 1981 or the BBC licence equivalent to broadcast news and matters of political controversy with 'due impartiality'. The ban was a barrier to such reporting which there were ways of negotiating; but as between the citizen and the terrorist there could not be due impartiality. The comments on proportionality, which as a discrete principle has undoubtedly influenced the interpretation of the Convention by the Court at Strasbourg as well as the development of administrative law elsewhere in Europe, also act as a corrective to Lord Donaldson MR's comment that 'you have to look long and hard before you can detect any difference between the English common law and the principles set out in the Convention' (*Brind,* op. cit, p. 477).

Similarly the invocation of Article 8 of the Convention did not assist an English court to establish the right to protection from invasion of privacy (*Kaye v. Robertson The Times* 21 March 1990). The absence of such protection in English law has undoubtedly been abused by irresponsible members of the press. A private member's Bill seeking to confer such protection in 1988 would have erred too far on the side of protecting the privacy of information as opposed to the public's right to know. The press have been allowed to regulate themselves where the law of confidentiality, defamation, obscenity, blasphemy, incitement etc. do not apply. A revamped Press Council under Louis Blom Cooper Q.C., established a code of practice with sixteen points of principle, including accuracy, opportunity to reply, protection of privacy and protecting confidential sources. The protection of privacy principle stipulates that the Council's Declaration of Principle on Privacy should be observed. The Council's powers are voluntary and inadequate. There has been a recommendation from the Calcutt Inquiry into privacy (Cm. 1102) for a statutory Press Complaints' Commission, possibly based upon the Broadcasting Complaints Commission. The press will be given a specific period of time to introduce a stricter and more detailed code of practice administered by a more powerful non-statutory Commission in order to avoid statutory regulation. The recommendation has been perceived by the press as ostensibly well-intentioned but nevertheless concealing the opportunity for political regulation of the press. For broadcasters, the Broadcasting Bill 1990 will allow the Independent Television Commission to fine persistent or serious offenders against their contractual codes.[10] The press had hoped that the installation of 'domestic' ombudsmen within newspapers, a new complaints procedure and pre-publication contact by the Council's chairman with editors, would ward off statutory regulation.

It would require a treatise on its own to unravel government use and manipulation of the press and media and the growing importance of the Prime Minister's press secretary in manipulating government information and public opinion. It is worth pausing a few moments, however, to examine governmental use of publicity to supplement traditional methods of information dissemination (and see Treasury and Civil Service Committee 1990).

Government Publicity

Unlike local government, central government publicity is regulated by conventions rather than law. Central government generally has rejected the case for legal regulation although, as the litigation involving leaflets advertising the poll tax in 1989 established, publicity is subject to the requirements of reasonableness and general accuracy; i.e. it is not manifestly inaccurate (*R v. Secretary of State for the Environment ex p. Greenwich LBC The Times* 17 May 1989: McGougan 1990).

Control over departmental publicity is exercised via the Cabinet Office for propriety, and the Treasury for value for money. Following disquiet and allegations that the Government's use of publicity to advertise and to sell its privatisation programme was for party political and not governmental purposes, the National Audit Office launched a widespread inquiry into expenditure on government publicity which in 1988-89 amounted to £200 million (National Audit Office 1989). The NAO considered that there had been significant improvements in the organisation and management of government publicity over the past ten years, but there had also been significant failures by departments to research the audience to be reached and how best to reach it. The Comptroller and Auditor General cannot formally rule on the legality of government expenditure but is restricted to examining its economy, efficiency and effectiveness. He cannot examine the merits of government policy. He did point out, however, that both the Independent Broadcasting Authority and the Advertising Standards Authority had criticised the terms of government advertising and publicity in the past. Even so, no evidence of breach of guidelines for party political purposes emerged. The Public Accounts Committee subsequently reported that Government needs to strive harder to ensure that its publicity campaigns are not politically motivated (HC 81 1989-90).

Apart from the Public Records Acts and the '30 year rule' there is no general right to information held by central government as opposed to local authorities. This point was recently emphasised by the Law Lords when the Secretary of State refused to publish the report of the Department of Trade and Industry inspectors into the takeover of Harrods by the Fayed brothers (Lonhro PLC v. Secretary of State for Trade and Industry [1989] 2 All ER 609; see Companies Act 1989 Section 151). The decision and the discretion to publish were the

Secretary of State's alone, even though the Divisional Court ruled that the refusal to publish cried out for justification. Unfortunately, there is no general duty to provide information or reasoned decisions in English law. The control by government of the flow of information and the cutback on statistics on, for example, economic indicators, industrial performance, or degrees and statistics of poverty, are therefore all the more serious from the perspective of informed debate and responsible criticism. The Chancellor of the Exchequer has also accepted that inadequate statistics played their part in the growth of inflation. The government statistics network, located in the Central Statistical Office, is answerable directly to the Treasury. The point has been made that while there is no evidence of rigging statistics by politicians, the UK system lacked the means and independence to withstand such interference.

At this point it is worth making an excursion to consider the law of a kindred democratic state which insists on the presumption of access to government-held information. The experience and difficulties associated with the US Freedom of Information Act (FOIA) may prove helpful in looking forward to a freedom of information future in Britain.

We have witnessed so far minimal concessions by the government in its 'reform' of the secret state and a complex and confused picture, or part of it, concerning the provision of information to the public and its control and regulation by judicial and administrative bodies. The US FOIA has many supporters in this country. However, the actual extent and nature of its operations are not so widely known. Nor are the problems, the real ones and not simply the perceived or exaggerated, which materialise with such legislation. In advocating a FOIA for the UK, we must be aware of, and learn from the country with the longest experience of such legislation in the English speaking world. Ideas are easier to import than legislation, and the US legislation was devised in a very different context to our own. Nevertheless, the operation of the legislation can teach us invaluable lessons in putting an idea into practice in a different cultural context.

The United States of America Freedom of Information Act
The United States Freedom of Information Act now in operation for almost a quarter of a century, is, I believe, a remarkable development in democratic government. Canada, Australia and New Zealand are closer to the British style of government and have adopted either the ombudsman/tribunal structure or both to resolve disputes over access to information. The US FOIA represents a struggle within government itself between the executive and congressional branches, and heavy reliance is placed upon the courts to resolve disputes. The US

experience can offer invaluable insights into the operation and difficulties associated with FOIA. In a common law system, it has the longest experience of such rights, and provides the most detailed instruction. After an initial period of public apathy, use of the legislation increased substantially after 1974. In 1990, for instance, the FBI reported a thirty seven per cent increase in workload for FOIA applications and spent $14,593,762 on its FOIA operation in 1989; about one per cent of its overall budget for the year (US Dept. of Justice *FOIA Update* Vol. XI, No. 1. p. 1 (1990)). To comply with the Act's requirements to the full on response times (see below) would require a 'massive diversion' of additional resources, the FBI said. The statement shows that the Act is onerous; it is not tokenism. Although, because of budgetary reasons, compliance with the Act may not always have been strictly adhered to, the FBI did its best.

The Legislation

The FOIA was enacted in 1966 (5 USC Code 552) amended overruling a Presidential veto and extended in 1974, modified slightly in 1976, and further amended in 1986. The Act covers all agencies and departments in the executive branch of federal government. It does not apply to the judicial or legislative branches of government, or to the President's immediate personal staff whose sole duty is to give advice and assistance to him. Every agency covered by the Act has to make publicly available in the Federal Register the following: information on its organisation; the places and persons from whom, and the methods whereby, information may be obtained. The Act provides that information must be provided on where requests may be made or where decisions may be obtained. The agency's decision-making and administrative processes, both formal and informal, have to be explained in detail for the public, as well as the agency's rules of procedure, forms and relevant instructions; the agency's substantive rules of general applicability adopted or authorised by law, and statements of general policy or interpretations of general applicability formulated and adopted by the agency must likewise be made public in the Federal Register. If the above are not published, then they cannot be relied upon by the agency in a manner adverse to the interests of an individual. Opinions, orders and staff manuals affecting members of the public have to be published, as do indexes of agency business, and are available in public libraries. Regulations are to be published by each agency with details of fee charges for processing requests. All agency records may be requested. Agencies must acknowledge a request within ten days, though the period may be extended. In fact a wait of several years is not unknown. The response must, of course, state whether or not the request will be complied with, and a further delay of ten days may be allowed for 'unusual circumstances', such as remote locations or substantial document review. If the agency does not comply it has to provide reasons for denial, and advise on administrative appeals. An appeal response should take twenty to thirty days. There is a *de novo* right of review in the federal courts, and the court may examine material *in camera* although such examinations are rare.

There are nine general exemptions, any or all of which agencies may choose to waive. (*Chrysler Corp. v. Brown* (1979) 441 US 281). The most important of these are: (1) material 'properly' classified by executive order to be secret because of national defence or foreign policy; (2) records related solely to the internal personnel rules and practices of an agency; (3) material specifically exempted from disclosure by statute, for example the CIA Information Act 1984; (4) trade secrets or confidential/commercial information; (5) inter or intra-agency memoranda or letters - an exemption which seeks to protect confidential advice in the decision-making process.[11] (6) information from personnel, medical and 'similar files' the disclosure of which would cause a 'clearly unwarranted invasion of privacy'; (7) records or information compiled for law enforcement purposes.

The FOIA does not define an 'agency record'. In fact 'a request may seek a printed or typed document, tape recording, map, computer printout, computer tape or similar item'. A request must 'reasonably describe' the record sought. Records are segregable, the non-exempt portions being publicly available. The burden of proof is on the government to justify an exemption.

The Privacy Act 1974 (PA) provides safeguards against invasion of privacy. The PA's intention is the converse of FOIA and seeks to restrict the use to which information collected about individuals by federal government may be put. It allows citizens to know how records about themselves, known as a 'system of records' because it is collected under a name, number, code etc., are collected, maintained, used and disseminated by the federal government. It also allows individuals access to most information maintained by agencies upon themselves with the right to seek amendment of any incorrect or incomplete information and compensation. The Act applies to agencies in the executive branch of the federal government and private bodies operating under contract with such agencies. Rights are given to US citizens and aliens lawfully admitted, but not to 'any person' as under FOIA. Exemptions apply, but no system of records is exempt from all PA requirements. Individuals may make requests for their personal files under both PA and FOIA since the exemptions are not identical.

The Government in the Sunshine Act of 1976 is an amendment to the FOIA open meetings law. It applies to meetings of agencies headed by a collegial body, a majority of whose members are appointed by the President with Senate approval. There are approximately fifty of these bodies including all the major agencies. It allows observation of, but not participation in, the deliberative process of government, although purely exploratory discussions are excluded. All FOIA exemptions apply except the one relating to inter and intra-agency memoranda. The Act provides the requirements that must be met to close meetings to the public, the amount of advance publicity that a meeting must be given and record-keeping. Judicial review of decisions to close meetings is available.

The Federal Advisory Committee Act, enacted in 1972, is similarly motivated. It regulates the formation and operation of advisory committees by federal agencies (Section 3). The Act requires that new advisory committees be established only after public notice, and upon a determination that establishment of a committee is in the public interest. Each advisory committee should have a clearly defined purpose and its membership should be fairly balanced in terms of points of view represented and the functions to be performed. To achieve a balance, 'agencies shall consider for membership a cross-section of interested persons and groups with demonstrated professional or personal qualifications or experience to contribute' to the subject (General Service Administration Regs., 1984, ch. 101-6 1007 (a) 2 (iii)). The status of, and need for, each committee should be subject to periodic review. Most importantly from the FOIA angle, meetings of advisory committees are open to the public, subject to the same exemptions as the Sunshine Act. Detailed minutes must also be kept.

The administration of the Act has not been without its critics, especially over the use of private sector groups as committees, *ad hoc* meetings of unstructured groups, and attempts at evasion. However, given the completely confidential protection afforded to most of the deliberations, and frequently even recommendations, of advisory committees in British government, and their inordinate influence in policy-making (Birkinshaw et al 1990), the Advisory Committee Act appears on the surface to be a remarkable development in open government.

The United States, then, has experienced the introduction and the strengthening of FOIA laws. It has also experienced a reaction against those laws. In fact, no statute governing federal administrative practice has rivalled FOIA 'as a source of controversy or target of reform in recent years' (Grunewald, note 13 below, p. 235).

Executive Retrenchment

The 1980s witnessed a growing tendency to secrecy in executive operations in the USA, most dramatically those covert operations carried out on the executive's behalf in foreign jurisdictions. A variety of statutes sought to reform aspects of FOIA, or ease its bureaucratic burden. There have also been spectacular uses of National Security Decision Directives (NSDD) (see Relyea 1988). These are secret devices used by the President to issue instructions to officials on security and intelligence and domestic affairs. The most famous concerned the directive authorising arms sales to Iran, and the activities of Colonel North in Central America, which were used to avoid informing Congress of those activities[12] contrary to the law.

Further changes have included Executive Order (EO) 12356 which has substantially increased, for the first time in over thirteen years, the scope for classifying documents as confidential, secret or top secret in the interest of national defence or foreign policy. The Order has authorised, for the first time, the reclassification of documents previously released to the public. Once classified, the documents are exempt from the access provisions of FOIA, although classification may be reviewed in the courts and is subject to a mandatory higher grade checking and administrative review/appeal, except where it is, basically, Presidential information. The Information Security Oversight Office oversees the operations of officials, and publishes an annual report. Where there is doubt about information, it is safeguarded as classified pending a determination within thirty days (Section 1.1(3) (c)). Further, the EO prohibits the use of classification to conceal 'violations of law, inefficiency, or administrative error; to prevent embarrassment to a person, organisation or agency; to restrain competition; or to prevent or delay the release of information that does not require protection in the interests of national security' (Section 1.6(a)).

NSDDs also authorise government employees' secrecy agreements. These cover, one commentator suggests, approximately 1.9 million federal employees (Katz 1987). Pre-publication agreements also cover certain officials, among them the CIA officials figuring in the Snepp case which was discussed above. Of course, there are legitimate reasons why secrecy agreements may be required, but the agreements are in terms which it is alleged oppose the legal rights of employees to 'whistle-blow' in the public interest. A Congressional statute with a provision preventing funds going to the President to implement such agreements was ruled unconstitutional insofar as Congress was trespassing into national security, the domain of the executive. (*American Foreign Service Ass. et al v Garfinkel* 87-2412-OG; *Nat Fed*

of Federal Employees v US 87 - 2284 - OG (DC); Pub. L No. 100-202 s.
630 (1987)). The voluminous case law in this area was dealt with in a
very cursory fashion by the court. A further development has seen an
extension of the ambit of the Espionage Act to cover leaks to the press,
and not simply spying as traditionally understood (*US v. Morison* 604 F
Supp. 655 (1985)).

Another EO has facilitated challenges by corporations to the
decision allowing access to information under FOIA requests which
those corporations have supplied to agencies on a 'commercial
confidential' basis. This is achieved by what is known as a 'reverse
FOIA suit': basically a judicial review on the record. The 'commercial
confidential' tag is now used routinely by companies supplying
information to agencies fulfilling regulatory responsibilities, such as the
Securities and Exchange Commission, the Environmental Protection
Agency and Consumer Product Safety Commission, as a means of
stalling a legitimate request which the commercial/confidential
exemption will not cover. But it neither creates nor extends an
exemption.

Last of all, Congress amended the FOIA in 1986. The
amendment expanded the exemption for law enforcement records
beyond investigatory files and was a response to FBI pressures. It also
excludes completely from FOIA requirements certain criminal law
enforcement records. An agency can, therefore, respond to requests
to see excluded files as if they did not exist. Even here, the
Attorney-General's Memorandum on the reforms advises on internal
reviews/appeals from 'no records' denials to ensure the correctness of
a decision. Internal audit is strict, in other words, although such
checking is not open to public scrutiny. Secondly, the 1986 amendment
altered the basis for charging fees. Three different levels of fee may be
charged. They shall be waived or reduced if disclosure of the
information is in the public interest, because it is likely to contribute
significantly to public understanding of the operations or activities of
government and is not primarily in the commercial interests of the
requester. Educational institutions, media and 'non commercial
scientific institutions requesters' are charged at the cheapest rate.
Commercial requesters are charged at the highest rate. Guidelines are
issued by the Office of Management and Budget (OMB) and,
controversially, the Department of Justice on the waiver provisions.
These set very stringent tests and provide for different categories of
user and fees. After an initial set-back, the National Security Archive,
a private organisation which collects unclassified and declassified
documents for public use on a non profit basis, was held by the DC

Circuit Court of Appeals to be a 'news media representative' but not an educational institution. They were therefore entitled to the cheapest rates of fee for their FOIA requests. The OMB guidance, however, was not invalidated (*Department of Defence v. N.S. Archive* 58 USLW 3596 (1990)).

The above developments should urge caution in describing the USA as a 'freedom of information' society. The inroads into the 1966 legislation have been all too evident. And yet the basic thrust towards openness survives and thrives. What impresses an outsider is the professionalism of FOIA officials in agencies and their acceptance of the culture of the Act and its requirements. The 1986 reforms, for instance, are accompanied by an Attorney-General's Memorandum advising that the reforms 'should be implemented carefully by all federal agencies possessing law enforcement information', consistent with the FOIA's mandate of achieving 'the fullest responsible disclosure'.

The Act imposes very different problems for agencies which vary enormously in their subject matter, size and organisation. Each agency is unique in that respect. The lack of uniformity in approach is evident in the fact that requests accepted by one agency may not be accepted by another.[13] However, it must also be borne in mind that different agencies have very many types and kinds of requester, from the highly professional to the bemused and indigent.

Responsibility for training rests with the Department of Justice. The Department organises regular conferences for officials throughout the United States on the FOIA and Privacy Act, publishes a highly regarded FOI Case List, which is a very detailed and comprehensive break-down of the legislation and its judicial interpretation, as well as the quarterly FOI Update. This latter publishes the names and addresses of all FOI contacts in government agencies, including the State Department, the CIA, National Security Council and the National Security Agency; in other words the sensitive agencies. A detailed instruction book for official attorneys and access professionals, giving a series of examples and working tests for those involved with FOIA, is published by the Department of Justice. Instruction is intensive, as not only are considerable employee hours involved in document search and review, but there are rights of appeal within agencies ending up with lawyer specialists in FOIA. These publicly available documents provide a valuable insight into official policy and thinking on FOI. One such example is the immensely important Vaughn Index.

Vaughn Index

Vaughn v. Rosen (484 F 2d 820 (1973)) established that in refusing access to information by relying upon an exemption, the mere *ipse dixit* of the agency is not sufficient to achieve exemption. An agency would have to furnish a detailed justification for exemption claims and would have to itemise and index the documents in such a manner as to correlate the justifications for refusal to disclose with the actual portions of the document claimed to be exempt. A trial judge can appoint a special master to examine the documents and to help him or her evaluate the agency's contentions (see *In re United States Department of Defence* No. 88 - 5044 (CA DC)). Vaughn represents a vital safeguard for a citizen in that the agency must make out a reasoned justification for refusal.

The practice has since developed of producing an 'oral' Vaughn affidavit. It is used to narrow the range of 'litigable issues' and to achieve an out of court settlement. In the words of the Attorney-General's manual:

> In an oral Vaughn proceeding, counsel for plaintiff and the defendant sit down with federal agency personnel familiar with the documents at issue. Plaintiff is then afforded a verbal description of the excised or totally withheld records and the Government's justification for those exemptions. It has been the experience of those who have utilised the oral Vaughn approach that it is frequently easier to present a clear description of the documents at issue in an informal setting where [the] plaintiff is present and able to ask questions as the conference proceeds ... the parties are free to broaden their discussions to include more than a strict description of withheld documents, and therefore, the oral Vaughn affords [the] department an opportunity to discuss exactly what has been involved with the processing of the request ... In addition, plaintiffs are often more willing to believe the Government's arguments concerning document sensitivity when meeting its representatives face to face. (Department of Justice 1987: p.V 57).

The guide goes on to offer examples of how such meetings have been used to reduce the number of requested documents from 'thousands to a few dozen' and how the meetings can be used as a forum for brokerage. For example, in return for release of documents covered in fact by exemption five - the inter and intra-agency exemption - the plaintiff would drop other requests; or the agency would release the identity of the source of information to the plaintiff, if the source was willing, providing the requester did not press for further release.

Grievance Redress

The involvement of the courts in *de novo* review of FOI cases is substantial; about 500 cases per annum each averaging eight months and costing on average $7,000. The vast majority are dealt with by summary judgment.

Judicial attitudes to the legislation have hardened in the late 1970s and 1980s. In 1988, for instance, the Supreme Court ruled in favour of an applicant for the first time in twelve years. The government prevails in just under eighty two per cent of cases going to final judgment. Nevertheless, one expert in FOI stated in evidence to a House Committee that the 'courts have interpreted a broad and vague statute into a manageable set of substantive procedural rules, generally in an independent spirit' (Grunewald, op.cit. note 13 above, p. 5.).

The Congressional sub-committee with FOI responsibility has conducted hearings into proposals for alternative methods of dispute resolution. The hearings were prompted by dissatisfaction with the role of the courts because of their expense and formality, and a desire for a more informal process to achieve effective resolution of disputes. Noting developments in Australia, Canada and New Zealand, as well as developments at the state level in the USA, the hearing took evidence about the desirability of ombudsmen and tribunals to resolve such grievances. The fact that difficult FOIA cases concerned an ever more detailed and time consuming document and index review prompted different suggestions as to the appropriate method of dispute resolution. From the government side there were assertions that the creation of a tribunal with binding powers to insist on production of a document would be unconstitutional as a negation of the separation of powers (S. Markman, Ass. Att. Gen. op.cit. note 13 above, p. 483). Other commentators felt that an ombudsman would simply be ignored or would be an unnecessary duplication. In fact the ombudsman concept has not succeeded in taking root in the USA (*ibid* pp. 476-80); not least, it is sometimes argued, because it is difficult to fit the office into a system of political trade-off and judicial redress.

Opposition, or a distinct lack of support for alternative modes of redress, came from lawyers representing a wide range of clients who felt that they could strike up a 'relationship' with agency lawyers whom they dealt with regularly (*ibid* pp. 107-12). They could bargain and engage in brokerage on an established basis; 'litigotiation' is the term sometimes adopted. Committees representing the press and public interest groups felt otherwise, supporting the existence of an ombudsman to act as a mediator and conciliator.[14] Interestingly, the Department of Justice, which processes appeals to the courts and assists agencies in FOIA litigation, has received and resolved complaints informally from citizens complaining about other agencies' treatment of their FOIA requests. The practice, involving a small number of cases, is not published or publicised. The Congressional Committee believed that the complete informality and institutional obscurity of such mechanisms made it impossible to evaluate meaningfully their success as complaint processors (op.cit. note 13, p. 335). In any event, government rejected any idea of an ombudsman or tribunal, arguing that this ran counter to the culture and traditions of U.S. Government.

User Groups

Over the years, a number of different interest groups have developed substantial expertise in FOIA: lawyers, the press (though only a small percentage of total users at between five to eight per cent (Birkinshaw 1988: 40)); public interest groups; scholars, and information agencies or retailers collecting and selling FOIA-acquired information commercially. Some of the public interest groups are highly professional and the National Security Archive, for instance, claims to have a more efficient indexing system for State Department documents obtained under FOIA than does the State Department whose officials use the NSA's library because it provides easier access to their own documents. However, the FOIA was never intended to be a 'hot news item' source of information. Nevertheless, a House of Representatives Hearing transcript of 1985, running to almost 1,200 pages, provided an exhaustive list of examples from environmental groups, media groups, civil liberties groups etc. illustrating the importance of FOIA in achieving, or helping to achieve, effective government, efficient government and an informed public better able to understand and make judgments about issues affecting the public weal (Freedom of Information Reform Act 98th Congress, 2nd Sess., House Com. on Government Operations (1985)). The success of FOIA can be gauged by the fact that every state now has FOI laws, though not necessarily with the same presumptive right to access as the federal model. Some state laws, e.g. New York, Connecticut, are far more detailed, however, than the federal model and more citizen-directed.

Congressional Oversight

Congress has a central role in oversight of the Acts. Copious details of the administration of FOIA are reported annually by each agency to both Houses, and the Attorney-General has to report annually on cases litigated. In a more general context, congressional committees are vehement in backing up their demands for agency information with the threat of contempt of Congress proceedings. Case processing reports of individual cases are also followed up by the relevant committees of each House.[15]

American government is built upon institutionalised conflict between the branches of government in a way that British government is not. The British citizen is perhaps more trusting of government, though not necessarily more enamoured with it, than his or her US counterpart. This distrust helped Congress to pass FOIA, partly because it helped redress an imbalance between Congress and the Executive, although the most serious rupture in relationships took place several years after the Act was passed and led to the strengthening of FOIA in 1974. That imbalance may not be fully redressed or redressable, but Congress served the nation well when it treated American citizens as responsible adults and passed the FOIA. Executive officials are quick to point out that similar legislation should apply to Congress and to the affairs of members of Congress and the judiciary.

The US experience shows us that freedom of information, however circumscribed, does not simply take place overnight. It takes years of training and practical application to develop the necessary expertise and skill. Although constitutionally the law has to be seen as the result, in part, of the separation of powers struggle in American government, the actual practice in the United States has provided us with a vast amount of information about very different sorts of departments and agencies, very different types of requests, very different kinds of problems. FOI legislation covering central government will eventually come to the UK, however long its introduction may be delayed. Before it does arrive, we must give thought to the form of the legislation and how it can best be implemented to achieve its objectives. The American experience might appear more pertinent as we move significantly along a path to more hived-off and 'independent' executive agencies, away from the traditional departments of state and ministerial responsibility. There is also much to learn from some of the weaker points in the administration of FOIA and, for instance, the lack of consistency in practices which was described above.

That said, the candour, professionalism and accessibility of the senior FOIA and PA officials with whom I dealt was extremely marked and has left a lasting and positive impression. What is more, user groups invariably had a respect for the professionalism of officials and for their ability to deal and negotiate rather than simply to act as wooden bureaucrats.

Conclusion

In 1986 the British Treasury and Civil Service Select Committee commented that the evidence it had received on minister and civil servant relationships in the UK did 'not suggest that the Government has made a convincing case against some form of FOIA' (HC 92 I (1985-6): p. XXX). Conversely, the Prime Minister remained adamant that a FOIA for central government was unnecessary. It would undermine ministerial responsibility, a constitutional doctrine which a large number of former colleagues of the Prime Minister might now want to re-examine and recast.

Recent figures show that the Canadian and Australian FOIA each cost £6.6 million approximately per annum. Even allowing for a 250 per cent increase on that figure for the UK, it would still be only one quarter of the amount spent on military bands in the UK (£62 million). It would pale into insignificance compared with the £200 million or so spent by government on informing the electorate on what the government wants us to know about them, rather than on what the public wants to know about government. The administrative and litigation costs of FOIA in the United States in 1988 amounted to between $60,000,000 and $100,000,000. Public relations exercises in the USA by federal government amounted to between one and one and a half billion dollars.

The government has had its chances in recent years to introduce legislation on freedom of information and privacy protection. These have been rejected, and we have been left with a hotch-potch, piecemeal, unsystematic state of affairs. On the other hand the opposition has promised a FOIA if elected to office. If that came about, we would then have to focus upon the practicalities, the indexing, the personnel, the places of storage, the extent to which policy documents would be available, the resolution of disputes over access and the scope of exemptions (Birkinshaw 1988: 221-35). Such an Act would put the 'reforms' of the OSA and SSA into perspective. A public interest defence would doubtless be added to the OSA as well as a prior publication defence. The intelligence service would be brought within the SSA and a fuller form of democratic accountability introduced.

The Brighton attack on Mrs. Thatcher's life and the murder of two of her close friends and confidants by terrorists would, understandably enough, instil in the prime minister, as in any rational human being, a security consciousness. The existence of the criminal law to punish disclosures of official information apart from espionage has been widely accepted. However, the 1989 Act is still not adequately focussed when seeking to protect information which can endanger the well-being of the nation and the public and not simply the government. The potential scope for the offences is still far too wide for a democratic society. After the notorious episode in the summer of 1990 when the Prime Minister's private secretary's minutes of the meeting at Chequers were leaked, revealing a discussion between the Prime Minister and six academics on the fallibility of the German character, the first reported reaction was to consider a criminal prosecution. Someone had to be punished for such embarrassment!

Even in a rapidly changing and ostensibly more pacific political environment in global relationships, few would question the legitimate role of, and need for, security and intelligence services. However, the need for their existence should not justify the absence of safeguards to prevent their remit being taken as a licence for excesses in an unbridled pursuit of certain individuals' interpretation of *raison d'etat*. There must be a role for democratic and not simply executive oversight.

Overseas models have much to offer. Even in the US, the CIA is still subject to FOIA and PA obligations, although the 1984 CIA Information Act exempts working or operational documents. It is worthwhile providing some figures on this most sensitive of agencies. In 1986, that agency received 1,526 FOIA requests,[16] 1,312 PA requests and 256 mandatory review requests under EO 12356. Under the 1984 Act, the agency has to submit 'semi-annual' reports to Congress which include median response times. For FOI cases in 1986 it was 3.24 months, as opposed to 9.2 months in 1985, a reduction largely due to the removal of operational files it must be said. In that year, processing of FOIA/PA requests amounted to '107 man years' for agents who would otherwise be involved with intelligence activities. Since 1975, the agency estimated (Bush 1987) that $36 million had been expended on information requests, and that it had collected $105,086 in fees, although unofficial scepticism was voiced at these figures. Many complain about the secrecy of the CIA (Johnson 1990), yet it is subject to federal law, it is subject to congressional oversight and it puts the secrecy of our own security and intelligence services into stark context.

Attempts have been made to diminish congressional oversight[17] of security operations and the US executive has been preoccupied with secrecy throughout the 1980s. Nonetheless, the processes of US government are considerably more open than are our own. Furthermore, the US government has survived and no national catastrophe has ensued. Naturally, FOI can be abused, but that is merely an argument for vigilance, responsibility and education, rather than for denial. Are we to believe that the British people are not mature enough to accept that responsibility? Can we not learn from overseas experience that as the second millenium draws to a close, FOI is a condition of citizenship. Membership of the European Community will perhaps ultimately determine the scope of our right to know how our system of government works.[18]

Section 2 OSA was a statement of imperial pride, social exclusiveness, the virtues of unquestioned tradition and culture and a resonant reinforcement of an antiquated *status quo*. A mature society has no need of such impediments but has every entitlement to a FOIA. In any event, I know of no cogent argument against it.

Notes

1. Defence and internal security; foreign relations; currency and reserves; maintenance of law and order; Cabinet documents; confidences of the citizen; official information used for private gain.

2. This was at a crucial stage in attempts by the Secretary-General of the UN to achieve an amicable settlement.

3. N.b. the role of accountants and disclosures in the public interest: Section 47 Banking Act 1987, Section 109 Financial Services Act 1986, Part II Companies Act 1989; and see Section 4(1) Obscene Publications Act 1959.

4. A civil servant, dismissed on disciplinary grounds, will usually receive accrued benefits under the Civil Service Pension Scheme. The Treasury has the power to withhold part or whole of the pension if a civil servant is convicted under the OSA of an offence for which s/he is sentenced to a term of imprisonment of at least ten years, or to a series of offences which have terms amounting to ten years or more. A civil servant may also lose his/her pension if the offence of which they are convicted is thought to have been 'gravely injurious to the state' or 'liable to lead to serious loss of confidence in the public service': para. 8565, Civil Service Pay and Conditions of Service Code.

5. General Communications Headquarters in Cheltenham, the government's global intelligence centre.

6. The Data Protection Act 1984 covers police files, but there are wide exemptions. Manual police records are not covered by any legislation. The police National Identification Bureau is the central repository. Police give information in relation to those applying to work with children and for national security references. Exemptions apply to the Rehabilitation of Offenders Act for such information (see Home Affairs Committee 1990).

7. Since the list of statutes was published at 108 HC Debs., col. 560, 2 January 1987 Written Answers, the following can be added: Section 82 Banking Act 1987, Section 174 Water Act, Section 19 Social Security Act, Section 19 Fair Employment (NI) Act, Section 57 Electricity Act, Section 182 Finance Act, Sections 75 and 86 Companies Act; all 1989 statutes. Each department's Establishment Branch will advise on whether other Acts are relevant to the work of the department. The reference to prosecutions was in relation to information received from individuals or organisations.

8. Its budget is significantly smaller than MI5's, although its staff estimate is 3,000; ie 1,000 more than MI5's. A proposed merger between the two bodies was discussed in *The Guardian* 13 March 1990. This would give the Prime Minister greater control via the security co-ordinator and the Joint Intelligence Committee in the Cabinet Office. GCHQ is not covered by the legislation. The 'inquiries' for vetting are based at the procurement executive of the Ministry of Defence. The use of security officials after their retirement by private security firms specialising in blacklisting for political purposes has caused controversy: see Linn (1990). On proposed changes in negative vetting, see: 177 HC Debs., cols 159-61, 24 July 1990 Written Answer.

9. Wallace was a soldier working for army intelligence and information in Northern Ireland. He claimed he was part of an MI5-inspired 'dirty tricks' campaign against Northern Ireland and British politicians; the 'Clockwork Orange' campaign of the 1970s. Mrs Thatcher repeatedly denied the allegations, but in January 1990 a junior Minister, and subsequently the Defence Secretary, admitted in the Commons that new facts had come to light (166 HC Debs., cols 110-13, 30 and 31 January 1990 Written Answer, cols 446-7, 1 February 1990). A Ministry of Defence report placed in the library of the Commons on 14 May 1990 established that ministers had, in the past, unwittingly misled the Commons because their advisers did not have the full facts at their disposal (172 HC Debs., col. 328, 14 May 1990 Written Answer). An inquiry into the circumstances surrounding Wallace's dismissal for leaking a document was conducted by David Calcutt QC. *The Guardian* of 18 May 1990 reported that essential

papers on the case had been destroyed by the Civil Service Appeal Board in 1986.

10. The influence of the Peacock Report on broadcasting in 1986, (Cm. 9824,) appears, as of writing, to have gained in strength. The Independent Television Commission will monitor contract compliance; the Broadcasting Standards Council will vet standards on sex and violence; the Broadcasting Complaints Commission will continue to investigate relevant complaints about broadcasting and there will be an enhanced role for the law of obscenity.

11. The courts have drawn distinctions between material consisting primarily of opinions or recommendations, and purely factual material; the latter are available; the former not. However, the courts have recently moved towards a test which asks whether the release of the material would tend to expose the agency's decision-making in a manner that would discourage candid discussion within the agency. Even factual material may be withheld if it might reveal an act of editorial judgment: *Dudman Communications Corp*. 815 F. 2d 1566 (1987); cf *Wolfe v. DHSS* 825 F. 2d 1527 (1987).

12. NSDD 159 of 18 January 1985. Covert operations have to be authorised by a Presidential Finding; i.e. a signed record. North argued that NSDD 159 removed the necessity of a Finding.

13. Some agencies, e.g. the FBI, have central indexes for primary records while others do not. There are different practices for processing appeals and for the location of records, e.g. locally or centrally. Research methodologies differ between agencies and 'remarkably, almost every agency resists describing the agency's search methodology to requesters'; FOIA: Alternative Dispute Resolution Procedures: House Committee on Government Operations, 100th Congress, 2nd Session, 1 and 2 December 1987 (1988), p.206.

14. Some of the official misgivings about the utility of an ombudsman may have been caused by the fact that the former Canadian Information Ombudsman was not allowed by the Canadian Government to testify upon oath on the record of the House Committee's hearings. She was prepared to give unsworn evidence, but the chairperson would not allow this.

15. The committees are the Sub-Committee on Government, Information and Agriculture of the House Committee on Government Operations and the Senate Judiciary Committee.

16. There were 850 refusals to comply with FOIA requests and 680 FOIA cases in which access was not granted or denied: e.g. no records existed, or the records were the responsibility of another agency to which the requester was referred, or the requester did not

respond to a request for further particulars. There were 95 appeals against initial refusals, 73 of which were completely unsuccessful, 22 partially successful ('denied in part'). 279 requests were granted in full, 406 in part: CIA, *FOIA Annual Report to Congress* 1986.

17. In the Iran-Contra debacle, the Congressional committee was misled; the Independent Counsel obtained the more damaging information.

18. Especially by the Directive concerned with access to environmental information; the Directive will require each Member State to introduce an access to environmental information act by 1993. There is a considerable body of exemptions: see the Environmental Protection Bill (UK) 1990. On the eventual EC Council Directive (90/313/EEC) see Official Journal of the EC L 158/56, 23 June 1990.

References

Aitken, J. (1971) *Officially Secret*, London, Weidenfeld and Nicolson.

Armstrong, R. (1985) 'Ministers, Politicians and Public Servants', *Public Money*, September, 39-45.

Aubrey, C. (1981) *Who's Watching You?*, London, Penguin.

Birkett, N. (1957) *Interception of Communications*, Cm. 283, HMSO.

Birkinshaw, P. (1988) *Freedom of Information: The Law The Practice and The Ideal*, London, Weidenfeld and Nicolson.

Birkinshaw, P. (1990) *Government and Information: Access, Disclosure and Regulation*, London, Butterworths.

Birkinshaw, P., Harden, I. and Lewis, N. (1990) *Government by Moonlight: The Hybrid Parts of the State*, London, Unwin Hyman.

Bolton, R. (1990) *Death on The Rock and Other Stories*, W.H. Allen Publisher.

Bush, G. (1987) Letter from CIA Deputy Director of Administration to George Bush, President of the Senate, 28 February.

Civil Service Department (1979) *Legal Entitlement and Administrative Practices*, HMSO.

Cripps, Y. (1987) *The Legal Implications of Disclosures in the Public Interest*, Oxford, ESC Pub. Ltd.

Department of the Environment (1988) *The Conduct of Local Authority Business,* Cm. 433, HMSO.

Department of Justice (US) (1987) *FOIA For Attorneys and Access Professionals*, Attorney General's Advocacy Institute.

Denning, Lord (1963) *The Profumo Affair Inquiry,* Cm. 2152, HMSO.

Frankel, M. (1990) 'Parliamentary Accountability', in N. Lewis et al (eds.) *Happy & Glorious: The Constitution in Transition*, Open University Press.

Franks, Sir Oliver (1972) *Departmental Committee on Section 2 of the Official Secrets Act 1911,* Vol.1, Cm. 5104, HMSO.

Fulton, Lord (1968) *The Civil Service,* Cm. 3638, HMSO.

Griffith, J.A.G. (1989) 'The Official Secrets Act 1989', *Journal of Law and Society,* 16, 273-290.

Home Affairs Committee (1990) *Third Report Criminal Records,* HC 285 (1989-90).

Home Office (1988) *Broadcasting in the 90s*, Cm. 517, HMSO.

Johnson, L.K. (1990) *America's Secret Power: The CIA in a Democratic Society*, Oxford University Press.

Jowell, J. (1990) 'Broadcasting and Terrorism, Human Rights and Proportionality' *Public Law*, 149-56.

Katz, S.L. (1987) *Government Secrecy: Decisions Without Democracy*, People for the American Way, Washington.

Leigh, I and Lustgarten, L. (1989) 'The Security Service Act 1989', *Modern Law Review*, 52, 801-36.

Linn, I. (1990) *Application Refused: Employment Vetting By the State*.

MacCormick, M. (1986) 'The Interests of the State and the Rule of Law' in P. Wallington and R. Merkin eds. *Essays in Memory of F.H. Lawson*.

McDonald, D. (1981) (1981) *Commission of Inquiry concerning Certain Activities of the RCMP; Freedom and Security Under the Law*, Ottawa, Canada.

McGougan, A. (1990) 'The Importance of Being Honest', *Media Law and Practice,* 17.

National Audit Office (1989) *Publicity Services for Government Departments*, HC 46 (1989-90).

Nicol, A. (1979) 'Official Secrets and Jury Vetting', *Criminal Law Review*, 284-91.

Ponting, C. (1985) *The Right To Know*, London, Sphere Books Ltd.

Relyea, H. (1988) 'The Coming of Secret Law' *Government Information Quarterly*, 97.

Stalker, J. (1988) *Stalker*, London.

Treasury and Civil Service Committee (1986) *Civil Servants and Ministers: Duties and Responsibilities*, H.C. 92 I and II, (1985-86).

Treasury and Civil Service Committee (1990) *Civil Service Pay and Conditions of Service Code*, HC 260 (1989-90).

Widdicombe, D. (1986) *The Conduct of Local Authority Business*, Cm. 9797, HMSO.

Williams, D.G.T. (1965) *Not In The Public Interest,* London, Hutchinson.

Winfield, M. (1990) 'Minding Your Own Business: Self Regulation and Whistleblowing in British Companies', *Social Audit*.

Winetrobe, B.K. (1989) *The Official Secrets Bill 1988-89* : *The Commons Debates,* Research Note No. 437, House of Commons Library, Research Division.